Systems and Software Quality

Martin Wieczorek • Diederik Vos • Heinz Bons

Systems and Software Quality

The next step for industrialisation

 Springer

Martin Wieczorek
Diederik Vos
Heinz Bons
SQS Software Quality Systems AG
Cologne
Germany

ISBN 978-3-642-39970-1   ISBN 978-3-642-39971-8 (eBook)
DOI 10.1007/978-3-642-39971-8
Springer Heidelberg New York Dordrecht London

Library of Congress Control Number: 2014939035

Printed on acid-free paper

Springer is part of Springer Science+Business Media (www.springer.com)

Foreword by Walter Brenner

Software Quality: An Evergreen of Information Management

Since the early days of my life, songs like "Yesterday" by The Beatles, "Satisfaction" by The Rolling Stones, "Comfortably Numb" by Pink Floyd or "Layla" by Eric Clapton have given me joy and calmness. It is not that I listen to them every day, but after a few beats I recognise them and appreciate the ingenuity of the musicians who created those songs.

Software quality is a topic that reminds me of my studies in the early 1980s, where program testing was on the curriculum. When I was working for a company in the chemical industry, software quality was one of my daily problems and tasks. Today, software quality is not the institute's research focus, but it is an area that continually challenges my work on information management, industrial services and enterprise systems, design thinking and digital consumer business. As with the evergreens, the same is true for software quality: after a few "beats" one is able to deal with it, to ask questions, to find defects and to derive risks.

One of the characteristics of evergreens in music is that they are made for eternity. A similar conclusion seems justified for software quality: as long as software is developed and maintained and subsequently used, we need to deal with software quality through quality assurance and testing. Every generation of software developers needs to learn about the importance of software quality and the complexity of achieving a high level of software quality. They also need to recognise and understand that strong and sustainable processes help to improve software quality.

To me it is clear: software and its quality will become a key factor in daily business and life. In the near future most of our products and services will depend on software. There will be virtually no products or services that do not have a software component, nor will there be any business or private processes that are not supported, managed or controlled without software. For every private and business question there will be an app to provide the answer. The next stage of development may emerge from embedded systems and sensors. Embedded systems are processors that are integrated, for example, in cars, planes, harvesting equipment and washing machines and that control them. Sensors enable us to get a digital view on the real world's state and conditions, e.g. room temperature and user's location, and to use this information for further calculations. Global networks interconnect individuals, companies and machines and enable the exchange of data and information. This new digital world functions because of complex software. Inevitably, software quality will be a key factor for many companies that are looking for differentiators for their products, services and processes.

In this book the three authors have taken up the challenge to investigate and discuss systems and software quality. Based on many years of practical experience gained from working for companies of different sizes and in different industries they provide an approach to professionalise the field of systems and software quality. The book is clearly structured and easy to read and recommendable for everybody who has responsibility in this area. The presented approach is pragmatic and helps to put comprehensive processes and governance mechanisms into practice. It is a great merit of the authors that they have developed an approach that takes into account both the quality of business processes and respective software systems and the quality of embedded systems. The authors' holistic view makes clear that integrated technical and economic management models will become even more indispensable in the future to ensure quality of all the software-based systems.

In the past I have seen many approaches which discussed software quality either of business software systems or of embedded systems. Usually people who are concerned with business software and embedded systems work in "separated worlds" inside the company. In the future they must work together because these two "worlds" are increasingly merging; consider, for example, new concepts like "remote monitoring". The holistic approach presented in this book is of great help in this complex learning process about software quality. In this sense, too, there is a parallel with evergreens: take, for example, a recording of "Satisfaction" by The Rolling Stones from the late 1960s and a recording of the same song from 2013 in Hyde Park. You will find that it is the same song text, but the sound has developed significantly since the 1960s. Just as it is gratifying to listen again and again to the evergreens of music, it will be rewarding to read this book and to rethink systems and software quality.

I wish the readers pleasant reading and the authors every success in the highly competitive book market!

Walter Brenner
Professor on Information Management,
Industrial Services, Design Thinking and
Digital Consumer, University of St. Gallen,
Switzerland
February 2014

Foreword by Wolfgang Gaertner

Testing and Quality Management in software development have become more visible and sophisticated in recent years. There is no doubt that professional testing and a comprehensive quality approach based on proven methodologies are key for successful software development. However, there is no "one fits all" solution that could be universally applied in every context. IT managers still face the challenge of defining a comprehensive quality framework that accounts for the specific environment of the business area, technology, culture, and quality needs of their respective organization.

This book shall be a manual on how to define and establish such a Quality Framework. Gain insights as to how a standardized software factory approach can unleash hidden potential and synergies. See how to approach the quality question on a strategic, tactical, and operational level by getting a notion of suitable software and systems quality. These topics are highly relevant to those who want to take a holistic view on quality and take appropriate action to achieve ambitious goals in a complex environment.

Looking at today's banking business we see constant changes in a dynamic market environment. Globalization and increasing regulatory requirements in all areas of banking are strong drivers for change. In order to compete in this dynamic and challenging market, financial institutions are continuously striving to provide state of the art products and services as well as to reduce their cost base by using a standardized IT infrastructure. Banking IT units are expected to introduce new and innovative technology and to speed up development cycles to allow for shorter time to market so as to support their partners in the customer-facing business areas.

Apart from the usual book of work, today's IT units may have a multitude of tasks and challenges, such as the integration of other financial institutions and the consolidation of IT platforms, to name a few. The acquisition and integration of Postbank and the implementation of a new joint IT platform for both banks are good examples for such a challenge at Deutsche Bank. In order to accomplish this task and the entailing changes, Deutsche Bank introduced the Magellan Program in 2011. Magellan will be completed in 2015 on the basis of synchronized software releases every half year.

In a program like Magellan quality is key for a successful delivery. The impact of the change on the end user and the software maintenance effort are considerable and meeting the quality objectives is extremely important. Quality measures applied in a large program are also a significant cost factor. To achieve the required quality in the most efficient way, Deutsche Bank established a comprehensive quality framework that focuses on items with the highest leverage.

The key factors we have identified and implemented in Deutsche Bank in large programs like Magellan are as follows:

- An obligatory quality framework to ensure standardized SDLC and quality management processes, methods, and tools—from front to back
- Stringent Release Management including Quality Gate control across overall project portfolio
- Integrated but independent Testing Utility acting as dedicated quality assurance function and gatekeeper for production
- Highly standardized tool setup and a comprehensive automation framework across the overall testing process
- Centralized test environments and test data management to guarantee a seamless start into testing activities
- Operational Quality Management for programs and projects to achieve the defined quality goals

In Deutsche Bank we consider the quality of our business processes a key differentiator in a highly competitive market and the underlying methodology is of utmost importance to us. The frame conditions are determined by today's development in the banking industry.

I hope that all professionals will benefit from the authors' ideas, i.e., to get new impulses to adjust or improve their IT processes and the quality of their software systems to the advantage of their business. Ultimately, I wish the authors to have interesting and productive discussions with the readers of this book.

Wolfgang Gaertner
CIO Retail,
Deutsche Bank AG Eschborn,
Germany
April 2014

Foreword by Ali Sunyaev

The importance of systems and software quality in the development and operation of information systems (IS) is undeniable. Successful accomplishment of IS projects is a crucial challenge for organisations and the high rate of problematic or failed IS projects is an ongoing problem. Despite several decades of research on this topic, there is still a lack of agreement on what factors lead to success or failure of IS projects. Important aspects of software quality are often not visible, and this holds for high as well as low software quality. Invisibility of high quality refers to missing acknowledgement of quality efforts since they might not be perceived and thus put into question. Invisibility of low data quality may encompass unconsidered costs of rework after deployment, future costs due to side effects, and low quality not directly visible for all users.

In order to examine what factors lead to successful IS projects and high quality software products, the University of Cologne, Germany, conducted an explanatory study, interviewing executives and IT experts in different organisations.[1]

As this book suggests, missing software quality is a *peccatum* and the level of quality is uncertain unless it is planned and controlled. The study shows shortcomings and pitfalls in both planning and control of software quality, and even the definition of software quality is a major challenge.

The definition of software quality is a challenge due to the diversity of quality dimensions, stakeholder perspectives, and project as well as organisational context. Moreover, software quality encompasses a process as well as a product perspective. Therefore, as suggested by the *four "P"s* concept, a holistic perspective of software quality within an organisation is necessary. The study shows that an organisation-wide quality policy, encompassing a holistic perspective, is a starting point for a common software quality understanding and embedding software quality at the strategic level. Additionally, a quality policy emphasises the importance of

---

[1] Paul Glowalla, Ali Sunyaev: Software-Quality-Governance, University of Cologne (in German only), February 2014.

software quality given time and budget constraints; a challenge that is addressed in this book as well.

In order to plan software quality it needs to be defined and should, as far as possible, be measurable. However, measuring software quality that encompasses the diverse stakeholders' perspectives is challenging, especially at the beginning. Few metrics are objectively measureable, like the number of defects, and even these numbers are subject to interpretation and so do not necessarily deliver a reliable assessment of software quality. Therefore, besides aiming at measuring software quality, qualitative measures need to be systematically established in order to communicate and learn from non-measurable aspects of software quality within and across potentially different IS projects.

Finally, high software quality is not an endeavour conducted at a single point in time. In order to control software quality, a continuous life-cycle is necessary to refine definition and planning of software quality and subsequently improve software quality and success of IS projects.

For long-term and sustainable software quality improvement, which might even require cultural changes, top management has central responsibility. Top management is responsible for establishing structures and responsibilities to allow for organisation-wide software quality awareness and assigning actions (top-down). Moreover, structures are necessary to allow for systematic learning from each IS project (bottom-up). Key Findings of the study are as follows:

- Quality responsibility should be differentiated into process and product quality, and a persistent delegation across organisational levels is necessary to enforce quality requirements within single projects while using gained experiences to learn across projects.
- A quality policy that increases awareness and facilitates common understanding to avoid diverging perspectives is needed. A quality policy links organisational culture and practices, but changes to culture resulting in practices might take time, since quality management is an educational process.
- Existing metrics are necessary for tangible project management and control and facilitate quantitative assessment of quality activities. However, if deviations occur, additional qualitative assessment is necessary. Since formalisation of project management might improve outcomes, qualitative measures should be formalised as well.

I recommend this book as a valuable resource. It provides insights into the systems and software quality field and inspires readers to adopt the suggested perspective on IS quality. I hope this book will find a broad dissemination and the attention it deserves.

Ali Sunyaev
Professor on Information Systems and
Information System Quality,
University of Cologne, Germany
February 2014

Foreword by Ina Schieferdecker

Cyber-physical systems (CPS) are networked embedded systems interconnected with cyberspace. In Europe, embedded systems are estimated to have exceeded the 10 billion mark. However, only a small share of these embedded systems is networked today. Yet, the interconnection of embedded systems by information and communication networks is growing rapidly. By 2020, there will be nearly 26 billion devices on the Internet of Things.[2]

The networking and interconnection of embedded systems impose new requirements and challenges for their quality engineering: The complexity, heterogeneity and dynamics of CPS in themselves and in the network of devices as well as their openness to cyberspace and their stringent requirements on functionalities, performance, security, safety and resilience call for new approaches regarding their constructive and analytical quality engineering.

Recent research in Germany, Europe and worldwide, for example in the Artemis projects CESAR (Cost-efficient methods and processes for safety-relevant embedded systems) and CRYSTAL (Critical system engineering acceleration), revealed new methods and tools leading to a reference technology platform for CPS. Selected results in quality engineering of networked embedded systems are presented in Zander et al.[3] Still, more research on quality engineering of CPS needs to evolve. But even more importantly, research results need to be transferred to the industry so that new methods, tools and processes can be adopted in daily industrial use.

It is a pleasure for me to present a prelude to this topical and interesting book on the industrialisation of system and software quality. The book reviews the state of the art in industry and standardisation and provides practical guidance on how to establish holistic quality management. Expertise, professional processes and automation are put into focus to master the quality of software-intense systems. By referencing elaborate technological results and best practices, the book presents a

---

[2] Gartner: "Forecast: The Internet of Things, Worldwide, 2013.", Dec. 2013, http://www.gartner.com/document/2625419?ref=QuickSearch&sthkw=G00259115

[3] Justyna Zander et al.: Model-Based Testing for Embedded Systems, CRC Press, 2011.

solid base for developing expertise and improving processes. A recent study by Fraunhofer FOKUS on "Status and Trends of Quality Assurance of Interconnected Embedded Systems"[4] revealed the increasing need for efficient and effective quality engineering. In the 2nd half of 2013, 19 interviews were conducted with quality managers in the automotive, avionics, transport, medical devices and smart grids industries. The interviews concentrated on product quality and quality governance, product and process quality assurance strategies, quality challenges of interconnected embedded systems and improvement requirements, potentials and options.

It was encouraging to hear that all companies see high value in product and process qualities. Clear structures and responsibilities have been established, although they differ a lot from company to company. Reviews and dynamic testing are integral parts of quality assurance. Yet, more elaborated technologies, methods and tools including, e.g., model-driven quality assurance, model-based testing, simulation or formal verification are not or only seldom in place. This could be one reason why more than half of the interviewees were not satisfied with the outcomes of their company's quality focus. Cost, resource and time limits are often not met because of quality issues. Moreover, many interviewees mention short-comings in requirements engineering and in component and system acceptance by vendors. The increasing networking, interconnection and openness of embedded systems are seen as new business-critical challenges. In particular, ICT security and privacy matters are of increasing importance and need to be addressed explicitly in quality management. In short:

- Many industries are currently focusing on product quality improvement of networked embedded systems. Therein, quality engineering for safety and security with respect to cyberspace is a major challenge.
- Product quality is seen in conjunction with own process improvements, process improvements with suppliers and advancements of the workforce. Continuous improvement approaches are often the basis for sustainable improvement effects.
- Ever shorter product release cycles and increasing complexity require new approaches in quality assurance. Agile, yet systematic methods in review and testing provide options for effective and efficient quality assurance.

Overall, the industry requires new approaches for the engineering of high-quality CPS. This book addresses integrated and holistic methods and processes for software-intensive systems. It describes a thorough quality focus and how to adopt the quality fabrication methods in industry. Although sophisticated quality engineering is not all about automation, much of it is.

Ina Schieferdecker
Professor on Model-Driven Engineering and
Quality Assurance of Software-Intensive
Systems at Free University of Berlin and at
Fraunhofer FOKUS, Berlin, Germany
February 2014

[4] Martin Schneider et al.: Stand und Trends der Qualitätssicherung von vernetzten eingebetteten Systemen, Fraunhofer FOKUS Study (in German only), Feb. 2014.

Preface

Software and systems quality is playing an increasingly important role in the growth of almost all organisations, both profit and non-profit. Quality is vital to the success of companies in their markets. Most small trade and repair businesses use software systems in their administration and marketing processes. Every doctor's surgery uses software to manage patients' records. Banking is no longer conceivable without software. Aircraft, lorries and cars use more and more software to handle their increasingly complex technical systems. Innovation, competition and cost pressure are always considerations in ongoing business decisions. The question facing these organisations is how to achieve the right level of quality of their software and software-based systems and products; that is, a level the market will reward, a level that mitigates the organisations' risks and a level the organisation is willing to pay for.

As in all industries, the software industry is subject to change driven from many fronts. New business models are created in response to new demands from different markets. New business processes are defined or existing business processes are adapted to changing business models. New solutions are built as new technologies become available. The changes in business and daily life but also the changes in the complexity and integration of software and systems are increasingly far-reaching. We believe that these changes have a huge impact on the art of development but also result in improved quality governance, quality management and quality engineering. It is not sufficient to define quality by budget and time.

The increasing integration of software as well as the search for suitable supply chain models in the life cycle requires appropriate quality solutions. Major sources for improving effectiveness, efficiency and reliability are re-use, standardisation, automation and specialisation as part of the industrialisation paradigm in the software industry. The rapid evolution of requirements due to new experiences, competition and cost pressure, but also changing technology such as mobile devices, has increased pressure on the software industry and its products. Likewise, there are impacts from new regulations issued by public and private authorities like Basel III, from a wealth of data and information overflow for users and providers and last but not least from new paradigms in the software industry itself like Agile development, which again pushes new and changing requirements.

For many decades software has occupied two different worlds: the "Embedded World" and the "ICT World" (ICT ≡ IT; although for the scope of this book, our preferred term is ICT). In our experience these two worlds behave differently in how they address the quality of the corresponding artefacts and final results. This book challenges this view and openly asks whether this coexistence and strong separation of techniques and procedures have a place in a future where globalisation leads to more integration and interoperability of formerly uncoupled or loosely coupled systems. What can we learn from both worlds and how can we apply best practices to improve enterprise ICT quality?

Although a number of good practices are in place, there is still room for major improvements. In our view, a holistic approach for systems and software quality is missing in ICT quality. Strategies and frameworks are required that will produce the kind of software and systems we need and we are willing to pay for. Let us therefore look at the two worlds of "Embedded systems" and "ICT systems" and learn from both worlds, from overlaps and individual solutions. Now is the time to take the next step for industrialisation in the software industry. With the aim of integrating a product and project oriented view on the ICT world, we will focus on three concepts in this book: (1) right software and systems quality; (2) industrialisation of quality engineering and (3) a holistic approach to enterprise ICT quality. As far as we are concerned, "Alea iacta est"—the die has been cast.

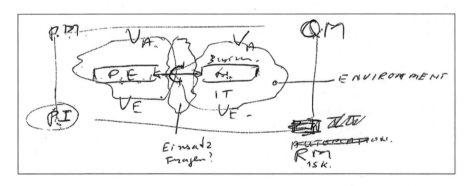

About the Book

Structure of the Book

As ICT should be an enabler of effective and profitable business today it is worthwhile discussing both aspects of an enterprise; we need to know the capabilities of ICT as well as the business needs. Therefore, our discussions in the next chapters will be along two lines. We will focus on ICT product quality improvements but also take into account the business demands.

ICT product quality is more than having testing processes and a quality management system in place. As already discussed by Heinz Bons, Rudolf van Megen and Peter Schmitz in their book "Software-Qualitätssicherung—Testen im Software-Lebenszyklus" (1982), every testing approach or concept has to answer these five questions when bug fixes, product changes and new products are implemented:

1. What are potential quality assurance and test items?
2. What has to be tested?
3. When should it be tested?
4. How will it be tested?
5. By whom will it be tested?

A quality management system defines and evaluates all the relevant processes. We also know that good processes are necessary but not sufficient to develop, maintain and operate ICT products during the whole life cycle. We believe that a holistic quality approach is needed in an enterprise and that it should entail a fundamental notion of right quality, an implementation framework and concepts and rules for establishing right quality across the strategic, tactical and operational layers.

This book is divided into eight chapters followed by two appendices and a glossary. The questions to be discussed and answered in the chapters are as follows:

1. **Motivation and introduction**. Why do we believe that a holistic quality approach will improve enterprise ICT quality? How do we assess the current situation of enterprise ICT? What can we learn from the embedded world?
2. **The four "P"s of enterprise ICT**. What are the fundamental cornerstones of enterprise ICT? Why is portfolio management worthwhile, along with quality governance, quality management and quality engineering? How to invest in the right projects?
3. **What is right software and systems quality?** What are the determining factors for right quality? What are the relevant quality characteristics? How can we define quality models alongside development and maintenance processes within the life cycle? Are quality characteristics independent of time and stakeholder expectations?
4. **How can we establish right quality for an enterprise?** Why do existing governance approaches not suffice in our view? How do we handle the demands of right quality across the various layers of an enterprise? How is portfolio management related to the business landscape at the strategic layer? Why and how is an application portfolio useful for the ICT landscape at the tactical layer? How does it benefit project execution at the operational layer?
5. **How can we implement a framework for right quality?** What are the fundamental components of our implementation framework? How do they contribute to a factory approach of quality engineering? How is our House of Quality defined?
6. **The Quality Services Factory**. What is a Quality Services Factory? What are the building blocks of a QSF? How can we set up and operate a QSF? What must a QSF take into account in relation to existing business units and ICT service providers?
7. **The benefit of RiSSQ, balancing quality and risk**. What is the benefit of our RiSSQ approach? How can we calculate the right risk/quality level based on time and budget? How do we balance cost of quality and cost of risk?
8. **Summary and conclusion**. What has been achieved in this book? How can we support an enterprise by establishing right quality and implementing a framework? What are the main aspects of a checklist?

Target Audience

This book discusses many different aspects of enterprise ICT and its quality issues. It defines the fundamental notion of right software and systems quality, provides a holistic approach of enterprise ICT quality that combines portfolio management with quality management and quality governance and delivers a framework for implementing right software and systems quality through an industrialised quality engineering.

As such, this book is targeted at senior management and board members who are responsible for business and ICT and for defining and providing appropriate strategies, values and directives. It is also targeted at executives responsible for implementing corporate strategies, especially the ICT strategy, and for creating optimal rules and conditions, infrastructure and work environment. They include division and department heads, directors of development, governance managers, portfolio managers, product managers, application and system owners, quality managers, process managers, project managers and test managers.

Testers, quality engineers, developers and others who perform operational tasks in the software and systems life cycle are also invited to read this book. We believe the notions and concepts presented here can contribute significantly to improving the quality of the life cycle artefacts and processes.

We recommend Chaps. 1, 2, 4 and 7 to all readers. Chapter 3 is mainly intended for executives responsible for defining suitable quality and risk models. Those who are interested in setting up and establishing a Quality Services Factory should also read Chaps. 5 and 6. Those who are engaged in quality engineering and need to define or adopt quality models should also read Chap. 2.

About the Authors and Contributors

Authors

Martin J. Wieczorek joined SQS Software Quality Systems AG in March 1995. Since then he has been appointed to various roles and responsibilities in the SQS Group, including Head of the "Telecommunications, E-Commerce, and Public" Business Unit, responsible for sales and delivery, Head of Market the "Public" Market Unit, responsible for business development, and "Research and Innovation" Director, responsible for service management and service innovation in the SQS Group.

He has over 30 years' experience in the fields of software and systems development, quality assurance and testing, quality and risk management and process evaluation and improvement. He is experienced in national and international projects and industries such as Telecommunication, Logistics and Public Sector including NATO. As a software engineer he also participated in international space projects like the D1-Mission in the German Space Operations Centre. He also has considerable expertise in training IT professionals and educating students at various universities. He still coaches students in their Bachelor and Master theses.

Martin Wieczorek received his Ph.D. from Radboud University Nijmegen, the Netherlands, in 1994 with his thesis "Locative Temporal Logic and Distributed Real-Time Systems—Specification".

Diederik (Dik) Vos has been CEO of SQS Software Quality Systems AG since October 2012. He is responsible for the company's strategy and the management of the Group Management Board, to which he was appointed in March 2011. Dik Vos started at SQS Group as COO, responsible for global sales and operations. In this role he focused on driving forward company growth and improving the global SQS Group's operational excellence. In 2013 Dik Vos took over the position of director of Thinksoft Global Services Limited, the SQS subsidiary focused exclusively on BFSI testing.

He has considerable expertise in the field of Managed Services, IT Services and Management Consulting. As an internationally experienced manager he has demonstrated an ability to drive change within organisations, developing them into profitable companies while increasing customer satisfaction. He previously held senior management positions at AT&T, Lucent Technologies, AVAYA and International Network Services.

Heinz Bons has been working in the area of Software development and maintenance for 40 years, mainly in the fields of quality management, quality assurance and testing. He gained detailed theoretical, operational and management experience in these fields. He is co-author of one of the first books in German on quality assurance and testing in the software life cycle (published in 1982).

After his studies at the University of Cologne he was a research staff member at the University, including the field of quality assurance and testing. He has been a specialised consultant in these areas since 1981. Heinz Bons is co-founder of SQS Software Quality Systems AG. He was Managing Director and Board Member of SQS for about 25 years. Today he is principal consultant at SQS and responsible for defining, implementing, coaching and improving processes, methods and techniques for testing as well as quality management and quality assurance.

Contributors

Kai-Uwe Gawlik holds a Ph.D. in Physics with a focus on experimental and solid state physics. He has worked with SQS for 17 years, currently as Global Head of Service Management responsible for innovation and industrialisation of SQS services and continuous consolidation of SQS PractiQ best practices. As a project lead Kai-Uwe has worked in small and large quality engineering projects for different industries. His responsibilities and tasks include setting up organisational units, quality management, technical quality evaluation, test data and environment management and testing in general.

Shan Rajegopal a Ph.D. in Business with a focus on operational research. He has worked with SQS since 2013 and is responsible for the set-up of a Global Project and Portfolio Management Practice. Shan is a trusted business advisor and one of the leading authorities in innovation, portfolio and execution management. He provides advice and support in innovation, portfolio investments and delivery management with value realisation for international companies in various industries to radically improve their performance. Shan is also a much sought-after international speaker and author of books.

Thomas Thurner holds a qualification in Electrical Engineering with a focus on Data Processing and Telecommunication. He has worked with SQS for 6 years and is responsible for the "Industrial Services and Solutions" Market Unit. Before that he worked for 19 years in various positions as Engineer, Project Manager and Division Manager in the field of automotive embedded systems. His spectrum includes the development and testing of (safety-related) Mechatronic Systems, Real-Time Operating Systems, Data Bus Networks, Quality Assurance and Fault Tolerant Architectures.

Detlef Vohwinkel holds a qualification in Business Economics with a focus on Business Informatics. He has worked with SQS since 1992 and is currently responsible for the "Process Intelligence" Competence Centre. He acts as a lead assessor in process evaluation and improvement and supervision of process changes for SQS clients. He is one of the founding members of the Test SPICE SIG to systematically develop and enhance the model for improving testing processes. He represents SQS in the advisory board of intacs for the development and quality of the SPICE and Automotive SPICE assessor qualification and is the SQS business liaison for SEI.

Top row, left to *right*: Shan Rajegopal, Kai-Uwe Gawlik, Detlef Vohwinkel, Thomas Thurner
Lower row, left to *right*: Martin Wieczorek, Dik Vos, Heinz Bons

It has been an excellent team approach. We are greatly indebted to Detlef, Kai-Uwe, Shan and Thomas.

Martin Wieczorek, Dik Vos, Heinz Bons

Acknowledgements

Unlike many other industries and their disciplines, Information and Communication Technology is a young field of research, development and practice. It has led and will lead to many changes in our business and daily life. In the beginning of the 1980s software testing was considered to be superfluous because of upcoming code generation tools and software quality was a strange notion. It seemed only developers had anything to do with testing. Some 30 years later we are in a position to write down our experiences and conclusions of over 7,000 projects in software and systems development, in quality management and quality assurance and in helping companies to improve both their ICT products and processes.

Once we had made the decision to write this book we needed to come up with initial ideas, hold brainstorming sessions and talk to people in the field to get a better understanding of the topics. We were fortunate to have the input of managers, directors and experts and their vision and determination to help us achieve our goals during the entire project. We are greatly indebted to Riccardo Brizzi, Sven Euteneuer, Kai-Uwe Gawlik, René Gawron, Ralph Gillessen, Gireendra Kasmalkar, Shan Rajegopal, Jürgen Stöterau, Thomas Thurner and Detlef Vohwinkel.

As more and more chapters progressed, reviews became essential to improve our lines and thoughts. At this stage, experts from business, ICT, quality management and quality engineering were involved to challenge our reasoning and statements with their experience and knowledge. We are therefore very grateful to Tom Arant, Axel Bartram, Jochen Brunnstein, Viktor Clerc, Phil Codd, Jürgen Diel, Ivan Ericsson, Ben Fry, Rajesh Gidwani, Martin Hamann, Johannes Kreiner, Sven Nordhoff, Sylvia Resetarits, Jeff Schmidt, Evan Sloss, Ian Spurs and Keith Yorkston.

Turning a document consisting of a few chapters into a complete book and getting it published need some final steps. First there is the task of thoroughly reviewing the complete text as to structure and content. We are greatly indebted to Ralph Gillessen, Jeff Schmidt and Phil Tomblin who took the time to make a final review and provided valuable input and feedback. Another task is to formally check references and links and improve illustrations and tables. Many thanks go to Verena Ruckes and Alexander Scheffer for their patience and cooperation in referencing, reviewing and improving layout, text, tables and illustrations.

In a project like this there are many discussions, conversations and informal talks with people who might be forgotten in the above acknowledgements. We therefore extend our gratitude to those colleagues as well. It has been an excellent team approach.

Tom Arant   Axel Bartram   Riccardo Brizzi   Jochen Brunnstein   Viktor Clerc

Phil Codd   Jürgen Diel   Ivan Ericsson   Sven Euteneuer   Ben Fry

René Gawron   Rajesh Gidwani   Ralph Gillessen   Martin Hamann   Gireendra Kasmalkar

Johannes Kreiner   Sven Nordhoff   Sylvia Resetarits   Verena Ruckes   Alexander Scheffer

Jeff Schmidt   Evan Sloss   Jürgen Stöterau   Phil Tomblin   Keith Yorkston

We are proud of what we and those who contributed to this book have achieved.
Martin Wieczorek, Dik Vos, Heinz Bons

Trademarks

The names of actual companies and products mentioned in this book may be the trademarks of their respective owners. We refer specifically to the following names:

- Airbus A380®
- APRESS®
- Architecture Tradeoff Analysis Method^{SM} (ATAM)
- Automotive SPICE®
- Avaloq®
- COBIT®
- CMMI®
- EFQM®
- FlexRay™
- intacs™
- ISACA™
- ISTQB®
- ITIL®
- Mercedes-Benz E-series®
- Mercedes-Benz S-series®
- Microsoft®
- NASDAQ®
- Photoshop®
- PMI®
- SQS PractiQ®
- SAP®
- Temenos®
- Test SPICE®
- TMMi®
- TMap®
- TOGAF®
- V-Modell®

Contents

List of Figures

List of Tables

Chapter 1
Motivation and Introduction

In ancient times, living and working was characterised by using what nature produced and provided. Our first technologies were fire and tools such as blades, stone axes, spears and lances of varying quality depending on the capability and skills of those who made and used them. Early memory and calculation tools known as tally sticks were used to record and document numbers, quantities, or even messages. Another early device is the Chinese Abacus for arithmetical calculations. In today's world we have become strongly dependent on technical systems and information technology. Technological progress has accelerated to the point that whereas historic innovations took hundreds, even thousands, of years, we now have the situation that technology can become outdated in as little as a few weeks.

As a relatively young industry, the software industry for many years has sought new methods, procedures, and tools to make software development less error-prone and more cost-effective. A lot of new paradigms have been invented, such as incremental and Agile development paradigms. Product as well as process quality have become equally important concepts. All in all, we believe that a next step is necessary to improve software development, or parts of it, in the broader sense. We cover this in our book by introducing our concept of holistic quality management, our concept of industrialisation of quality engineering, and by defining the notion of right quality.

The following sections will motivate our approach by discussing interesting similarities and differences between the embedded and the ICT world. Section 1.1 motivates our approach and the content of this book. We look at real examples where systems have failed and discuss major challenges that have to be taken up and resolved. Section 1.2 provides a short historical view on information systems and embedded systems, and compares typical system characteristics from both worlds. Section 1.3 discusses industrialisation as a management concept for the software industry with special focus on quality engineering.

M. Wieczorek et al., *Systems and Software Quality*,
DOI 10.1007/978-3-642-39971-8_1, © Springer-Verlag Berlin Heidelberg 2014

1.1 Missing Software Quality, A Peccatum

ICT quality is free, as it is built into the product during development and maintenance. But the level of quality is uncertain unless specific actions are taken to plan
and control it. We will call such quality coincidental. In contrast, right quality is not
free but right quality differentiates in a highly competitive market. When we look
around us, in our daily work and business, we find considerable misconceptions.
Many expectations are raised about what ICT systems quality is and should be and
how quality management and quality assurance can contribute to the quality of
software and systems in the lifecycle. Although much progress has been made
during the last thirty years in software quality, too many of today's software
projects still struggle to achieve the right balance between time, budget and quality.
Given software and systems quality in a given environment results in a level of risk
of which the system owner must be aware. To the extent that the environment is
stable, the only parameter to control risk is quality, which again is dependent on
budget and time.

Let us discuss a few examples of software-based systems that failed and where
the failure had a huge impact on the company's image, products, and/or budgets or
on the customers and users of such systems.

1. **Example taken from (Russolillo** 2012**):** *"On August 1, 2012, the New York
   Stock Exchange (NYSE) has determined to cancel all trades of six symbols. "The
   trades executed 30 % or more above or below the opening price today between
   09:30:00 a.m. and 10:15:00 a.m. ET will be busted. This situation is still under
   review by all relevant regulatory authorities", NYSE said. Earlier on that
   Wednesday, NYSE Euronext told traders it was reviewing trades in 148 symbols,
   executed between 9:30 a.m. and 10:15 a.m. Eastern Time. Knight Capital
   Group, a trading firm, told customers to send orders elsewhere and said it
   was probing a software problem that affecting trading today. Shares went
   down 27 % to $7.51."*

   Discussion: This example shows the globalised impact of a failing system. It
   was reported that the issue above was caused by someone investigating a
   software problem. Why would someone be allowed to investigate a software
   problem by trial and error in a production environment? An environment,
   moreover, where everyone should know that this could have a direct impact on
   the daily business? What is more, this happened within a very short period of
   time, with trades being executed at 30 % above or below the opening price!

2. **Example taken from (NHTSA** 2012**):** *"BMW recalling 7 series models over
   unintentionally opening doors. There were totally 7.485 sedans involved in this
   software problem. The problem was found in Japan in 2007, covering cars from
   2005 to 2007 model years, and it led to recall. After the Japanese recall, the
   NHTSA asked about this matter in the United States in 2011. BMW replied that
   80 % of the cars replaced with new software. After conference with the German
   company, BMW announces about this recall issue in October, 2012."*

Discussion: It was reported that a software problem had occurred. But did they really know it was a software problem rather than a problem of the wrong requirements implemented in the right way? Did they define the requirements for opening doors beforehand in a complete and consistent manner? From our viewpoint, it is not clear whether the cause—not the trigger—was a software problem in the sense of wrong software code.

3. **Example taken from (Lever** 2012): *"Computer problems drew complaints across the US during the 2012 elections, with numerous problems with voting machine glitches reported by voters. An example was touchscreen errors automatically changing the vote from one candidate to another and not allowing voters to reselect or correct the error."*

   Discussion: This example mentions computer problems and not software problems. At first glance it seems to be a hardware problem relating to the touchscreens. But also in this case, it is not clear what caused the problems. Although the issues do not appear to be immediately relevant on a global scale, they could have consequences for democratic decisions and political behaviour and this is highly relevant in a democratic society.

4. **Example taken from (Linsky** 2012): *"For the third time in 2012, a computer glitch wreaked havoc on thousands of travellers with a US airline, delaying flights for hours. A glitch in the dispatch system software resulted in hundreds of delayed flights across the US and internationally. The 2 h outage held up 636 of the 5,679 scheduled flights and resulted in 10 flights being cancelled altogether."*

   Discussion: Financial loss and damage to the airline's image were the direct impacts in this example. Why had they not found the cause of the failure earlier? Why did this glitch occur three times in one year? Was it due to budget or time constraints? Did management decide not to invest in error detection and bug fixing?

5. **Example taken from (Gibb** 2012): *"A gambler, who was under the impression he'd won just over $1 million, was told by a High Court that, despite his anticipated windfall showing in the online game he had played, he was not a millionaire after all. A software error mistakenly reported his winnings as much higher than they actually were and, due to this contingency being covered in the game's terms and conditions, he could not legally claim his anticipated prize."*

   Discussion: It was reported that a software error mistakenly indicated the winnings. Again, it is not clear whether this was a software error, as it could have been a wrong text in a database table or a wrong requirement. The gambler must have known that messages generated by gaming software during execution are not always reliable and that the content could not be legally claimed, as terms and conditions usually exclude a lot of responsibility. So, it is easy to start a game but it could have consequences involving significant amounts. Do we have the right culture to handle such situations?

6. **Example taken from (Webb** 2012): *"An Australian energy company sent thousands of customers late payment charges for bills they didn't receive due to a computer glitch, while a German utility company overcharged 94,000 of its*

customers due to a computer glitch that incorrectly charged exit fees, costing the energy supplier $2.24 million in settlement pay-outs."

Discussion: Yet again, the reasons for the glitch are not apparent and the impact was huge; i.e. financial loss and reputational damage. The question again is why had they not found the cause of the failure earlier? Was it due to budget or time constraints? Did management decide not to invest in error detection as early as possible?

7. **Example taken from (Zappone** 2012): *"A leading multinational corporation's cloud computing service outage, which affected Governments and consumers, was caused by the additional day in February 2012. The same leap year date bug also affected an Australian payment system used by the health industry, resulting in 150,000 customers being prevented from using private health care cards for medical transactions for two days."*

Discussion: The leap year date phenomenon is well-known in the software industry. It is a fairly simple test to rule out a software error. Why was this error not found earlier? Again, was it due to budget or time constraints? Did management decide not to invest in error detection?

So far we have discussed a number of examples where defects occur repeatedly. For many years, different research reports have presented such examples, evaluated them and provided statistics. Although companies might suffer from customers switching to another company and their products and services we find that those companies are increasingly accepting these problems as long as there is the possibility of repairing all the defects in a production environment. The reasons are manifold; often we find complexity, political behaviour and lack of sustainability topping the list. It could cast a damning light on the software industry if software is mentioned as the reason for failure. This is not acceptable and in our view it can be mitigated and resolved.

In analysing the causes for such quality gaps it is helpful to differentiate three main categories: (1) real defects caused by errors made during software development; (2) those originating in misconceptions and incorrect designs; and (3) those originating in misunderstanding users' needs and requirements. There is another category, namely defects relating to aging of the corresponding system/product or parts of it.

1. **What you designed is different from what you get:** e.g. the design documents are ambiguous, which gives the software engineer a certain degree of freedom; or technological constraints restrict the software engineer in developing and implementing the corresponding software.
2. **What you require is different from what you design:** e.g. the requirements are ambiguous and the architect has some freedom in decisions; or environmental constraints lead to designs different from what is required.
3. **What you need is different from what you require:** e.g. the specified requirements do not or only partly reflect the real needs; requirements are not specified correctly due to user needs; or requirements are missing completely.

Acceptance of less than optimal quality seems to be widespread. Often we hear "yes, it has caused problems, but we accept it" or "yes, business was disrupted for a time with financial loss and harm to our image, but we accept it" or "yes, there was a threat to life or physical integrity, but we accept it because there was no other option". All this is often accompanied by inadequate communication to the company's stakeholders, both internal and external. It seems to be passed off as a law of nature. In the realm of risk management, risk acceptance seems to be a matter of choice, although everybody knows that it could be an expensive one. This is in spite of the existence of quality engineering, a discipline that provides solutions for transparency, predictability and links to business continuity. Not dealing with quality in the right way is a peccatum, i.e. a sin, as such systems will take over more and more responsibility for decisions that will guide and attract us.

In conclusion, it is clear that what we get is often not what we really need in our daily business and life. The reasons are manifold. Especially in sequential development models, there is a non-responsive gap between requirements definition and solution delivery. During this time span the business world will have changed; often the users will have changed and risks and opportunities will have changed too. In our view there are seven topics, or "sins", known from the past which are challenges for the future in the lifecycle of software-based systems.

1. *End-user needs and requirements:* Do the end-users know what support they need from an ICT or embedded system in their daily business or life? Yes, most often they do know but the challenge is to get this out of them. It is the "dilemma of the key player"—they have the knowledge but they are the least accessible. A further challenge is to make the requirements complete and consistent when they are documented. This is operational work and there are methods, procedures and tools to solve this. But what is still missing is traceability from needs to requirements, to business processes, to system components, and to verification and validations assets.

2. *Planning vs. governance:* Planning at the strategic, tactical and operational layers of a company is important and necessary. For example, estimating the time needed for a project, or the number of resources, or the budget, seems simple but is in fact complex. Finding a suitable work breakdown structure is crucial for every project management process to run effectively. Quality, in fact, is planned bottom up. Suitable demands are not given at senior levels. Very rarely are all aspects of a project known in the planning stage, but arise instead during execution. As we cannot predict all events and circumstances, we have to allow uncertainties in planning but we also need a good governance structure at all levels in a company. In this sense we often see too much planning and too little governance exercised in practice.

3. *Culture of collaboration and failure:* Often organisations exhibit behaviours that are not suited to resolving risks. Sometimes it is easy to get the impression that different stakeholders participating in projects and meetings are more interested in politics and their own agendas than working together towards

success. This is often underpinned by not being able to constructively handle failure and lack of quality. There is a fear of reporting matters that might affect planning and time-to-market issues in a counter-productive way. But, is it not the case that the sooner we know about problems and risks the more effectively we can respond to them?

4. *Problem solving by outsourcing:* Our experience suggests that organisations learn how to resolve their deficiencies quicker when they outsource parts of the business or the ICT. This is because processes and interfaces to the outsourcing partners have to be sound and clear. Outsourcing is driven by saving costs. But these cost-savings are not achieved just by transferring work to low-wage countries and changing contracts. Watertight definitions and contracts alone will not prevent software from failing. Organisational and process change also needs a prerequisite for success. A certain "maturity of the whole organisation" is needed. This maturity and the total costs of outsourcing are often underestimated. This is true for development as well as for quality assurance and testing.

5. *Budgeting:* ICT budgets are typically predefined for the next reporting period depending on the budget for the whole company. The assignment of particular budgets is most often based on high level decisions. For example, a client of ours was deliberating whether to invest in an expensive or a cheaper tool. They initially opted for the cheaper tool. We then did some cost-benefit calculations. A comparison of the different tools in the market showed that there was a really good tool which could fulfil the required properties but it was the most expensive one due to the number of licensees required. Considering only the investment and the static characteristics of the tools while neglecting the efficiency of its use during the whole lifecycle of its application led to a different ranking. The same is true when a project decides not to invest in automated regression scripts because the Return on Investment is beyond the life of the project. This then hampers the Operations team, who have to support and maintain the system throughout its lifecycle. This short-sighted decision leads to a much higher Total Cost of Ownership! What is the right budget? What are the determining factors? Is it a good idea to restrict project success without considering subsequent lifecycle costs caused by poor quality of the project's results?

6. *Portfolio management:* Two application areas of portfolio management have to be distinguished: one dealing with projects and programmes and the other dealing with applications, software and systems. Whereas the first category is mostly implemented, the second is often neglected. Remember the Y2K problem. Almost every big company whose business was highly dependent on hardware and software started a project to get transparency on its risk status for Y2K bugs and to solve these risks. Time-consuming and expensive actions had been taken to setup an inventory of all the systems. In hindsight, it was said that "too much effort and money had been spent, as it proved not necessary". First of all, such a statement is retrospective because effort and money had already been spent. Second, it might be that in some cases too much effort or money had been spent, but more importantly the inventory and all the

consolidated findings were no longer used after Y2K. An existing system portfolio management could have been the way to save the Y2K inventory results for future strategies, tactical planning and operational work. So, the challenge is to define and apply adequate portfolio management in a company to ensure reuse of assets across projects, programmes, portfolios, divisions, etc.

7. *Industrialisation:* Industrial processing has gained in importance for many sectors. In the software sector, industrialisation often means automation and tooling or outsourcing. Is this enough? Independent of the type of project and the particular tasks, software development is still a form of art work. So we need a suitable model for industrialisation and we need to implement this in organisations by means of process- and product-orientation (cf. also (Mellis 2001)). Furthermore, we need a notion of Right Software and Systems Quality to assure effective industrialisation. Otherwise it would be detrimental to our business, our companies, and possibly our society.

It seems that the software industry is focusing mainly on industrialisation to resolve the above-mentioned challenges. So, industrialisation today is most often associated with the following five dimensions cited in (BITKOM 2010) (cf. Fig. 1.1):

- **Reuse**, software components as part of libraries, frameworks and service repositories are provided for use in various environments;
- **Standardisation**, applying standards in the sense of modelling concepts and development platforms;
- **Specialisation**, due to complexity, technology lines and product lines are the main drivers for specialisation in software development and improving cost effectiveness;
- **Automation**, to support different tasks and activities two tool strategies are well-known and applied; i.e. the best-of-breed strategy, where tools are loosely coupled in a tool stream, and the best-of-suite strategy where one complete platform covers many aspects;
- **Continuous improvement**, improvements without knowing the current state of an organisation are not possible; also, it is inefficient to improve only once, so an organisation has to be evaluated continuously through assessments and measurements of the software-based systems and ICT processes.

Companies that systematically apply industrialisation in all these dimensions have the potential to achieve significant improvements. It will impact on a company's productivity. Maximising the value of core systems and their development processes is also an excellent starting point for outsourcing in order to further improve the cost-benefit ratio.

We believe that industrialisation alone is not the best solution. With ICT and ICT projects presenting such a major investment, a holistic approach must be defined and deployed so that goals and objectives, investments and benefits can be fully realised. Further trends of large-scale outsourcing and sub-contracting on all ICT projects increase the risk significantly. This puts an even bigger burden on

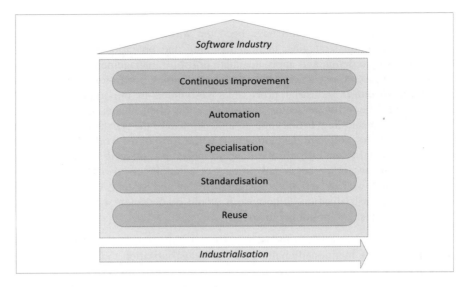

Fig. 1.1 BITKOM industrialisation dimensions

executives to take more responsibility and accountability for the actions and deliverables of their own staff, vendors and suppliers. Outsourcing can create a well-disciplined business relationship for delivering ICT components and services, but does not guarantee that the business will get what it needs from ICT, nor will outsourcing make sure business benefits are fully realised. To go back to the situation outlined above, confessing one's "sins" may relieve but not resolve any of the problems!

We believe that focusing more on quality issues in a holistic, business-driven quality approach will help organisations to achieve the optimal structure for the whole organisation, while avoiding neglect of projects or particular applications. More emphasis has to be placed on the quality of products; i.e. ICT and software-based systems. This is only possible if all three levels of an organisation, i.e. strategic, tactical and operational layers, are involved in the corresponding quality issues.

We believe that three pillars are needed to provide the next step for ensuring and improving quality of business through ICT:

1. An enterprise-wide concept integrating portfolio management, quality governance, quality management, and quality engineering;
2. An industrialisation model for quality engineering as implementation framework; and
3. An enterprise-wide notion of a right level of software and systems quality.

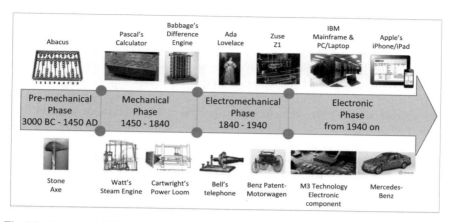

Fig. 1.2 Evolution of ICT and embedded systems

1.2 Information and Communication Technology

The beginning of information and communication technology—although the term itself was not used in those days—dates back to 3000 BC, maybe earlier, when writing in its widest sense was developed to store, retrieve, manipulate, and communicate information. Following (Butler 2012), four phases can be distinguished in the development of information technology and systems (cf. Fig. 1.2).

During the "pre-mechanical phase", from 3000 BC until 1450 AD, pictures, drawings, languages and alphabets came into existence. In this time period, the first numbering systems appeared and tools like the Abacus were used to perform calculations. The main characteristic of such systems is simplicity; i.e. only a single function is provided. Between 1450 and 1840, the "mechanical phase", a large number of technical systems, like steam engines and power looms, were invented. The foundation for book publications was laid with Gutenberg's invention of the metal-type printing process, which is also known as the first information explosion. Blaise Pascal, with his "Pascaline", and Charles Babbage, with his "Difference Engine", represent the next steps towards modern computer systems. This is when we see machines take over more complex tasks from humans. Between 1840 and 1940, called the "electromechanical phase", the foundation was laid for modern information and communication technology. It was the time of Alexander G. Bell, who invented the telephone (the "C" in ICT), and of Konrad Zuse, who invented the first computer Z1, and the first programmer, Ada Lovelace (together, the "I" in ICT). The next phase, known as the "electronic phase", started in 1940 and is still ongoing. In this phase more and more ICT and embedded systems were and are being invented by many different people.

Starting from the first modern computer, Zuse's Z1, information and communication technology has become more and more complex and distributed. The basic principles of the technology have not changed. We still have microprocessors and storage and communication devices. What has changed is the number of these components, their interconnectedness, and the algorithms of the various systems. Since then, different systems such as mainframes, personal computers, internet, and mobiles have been invented to make life and business more comfortable and efficient. Where a mainframe computer provides computing power for whole organisations and their tasks, the PC provides computing power to one individual. The internet allows interconnecting PCs, people and organisations to fulfil their tasks. The advent of wireless communications means individuals and organisations no longer need to be at a fixed location to be interconnected.

Consequently, the boundaries between technical systems, embedded systems and ICT systems have become blurred. Take as examples infotainment systems in cars, health care systems for patients or traffic control systems to keep traffic flowing. Other examples, like electronic trading systems on stock exchanges, warehouse management systems or hospital information systems, are explicitly included. It is the time of Rick Belluzzo, who in a speech in 1996 as executive Vice President and general manager of Hewlett-Packard said we have reached "the stage when we take computing for granted. We only notice its absence, rather than its presence". Others who argued in the same direction are Mark Weiser (Weiser 1991) and Friedemann Mattern (Mattern 2008).

Today's systems supply people, organisations, societies and other systems with information, which they in turn use to perform a particular task. From a user's perspective such systems are designed to collect and provide information or they are designed for performing a particular task, which they can do faster, more repeatedly or enable in the first place. We then expect a certain level of quality from those systems so that we can rely on the system's performance and information provided to get the right solution for a particular task. An example of the latter is "driving from A to B within a certain amount of time". In the 1960s this was called "trustworthiness of systems" (Boland 2010). Do we have it today where topics like privacy, security, safety, integrity and provenance of data are more relevant than ever?

Software-Based Systems

Many terms and phrases have appeared in theory and practice, in scientific publications and in marketing material. Think, for example, of terms like "pervasive computing", "ubiquitous computing", "wireless sensor networks", "embedded systems", "ICT systems", "computer systems", "computing systems", "smart grid", "autonomic computing"—you name it. A user perspective is at the same time a quality perspective. Both perspectives expect reliable and correctly functioning systems. What are the right notions and concepts to ensure trustworthiness? And how can we get a clear and sound understanding of the relevant properties and an authoritative assessment of trustworthiness?

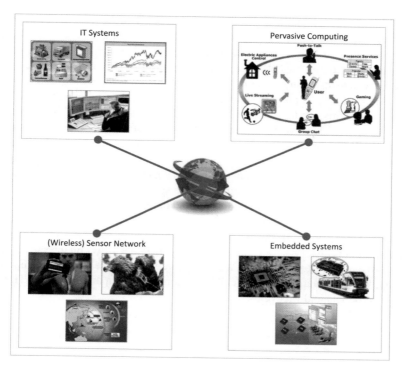

Fig. 1.3 Web-based electronic ecosystem

In this first chapter we differentiate between the ICT world and the embedded world to learn best practices from both worlds and to define quality notions for present and future ICT systems. The ICT world is a digital world, where software is the focal point, assuming that the underlying hardware, middleware and user interfaces are all functioning correctly as an assemblage of components. The embedded world is a hybrid one consisting of both digital and analogue components, but also uses software which is often—but not always—embedded in the memory of the processor board. The electronic world of today and the future combines ICT and embedded systems into one web-based electronic ecosystem consisting of many diverse, globally interconnected and sometimes autonomic systems (cf. Fig. 1.3). To give an idea about the evolution of this ecosystem: Machina Research expects the total number of connected devices to grow from 9 billion today to 24 billion in 2020, with half of these incorporating mobile technologies (cf. GSMA 2012).

Since the 1990s, Wireless Sensor Networks have become a prominent infrastructure to monitor and control the environment (cf. Dargie and Poellabauer 2010). Examples are structural health monitoring, traffic control, health care, pipeline monitoring and underground mining. Basically, these belong to the embedded systems world. From a quality perspective the following are important aspects:

the ability to cope with node and communication failures, the mobility of nodes, the ability to withstand harsh environmental conditions and the ease of use. Another type of system, in Fig. 1.3, is called pervasive (ubiquitous) computing. It is an advanced computing concept where "all data and information is available always and everywhere using information and communication technology" (cf. Weiser 1991; BSI 2006). Examples are smart grid, smart home, e-commerce, intelligent car assistance systems, smart cards and electronic identification cards. The other two categories in Fig. 1.3 will be discussed below in more detail. From a technology viewpoint, ICT and embedded systems are the basic concepts behind all the mentioned examples.

Quality is vital to people, organisations and societies. Obviously, those systems give us more information, more comfort, more speed, more mobility and so on; for example, think of big data, cloud, and apps. Therefore, we need to ask ourselves whether the concepts, methods, procedures and tools are still the right ones or whether we need to think more holistically about such systems. Most often the differentiation is history-based and reflects only different views on the same kind of objects. We need system quality as a driving force and differentiator in competitive markets, which is manifested vertically and horizontally in an enterprise. Think in terms of products and lifecycles.

ICT Systems Today

Generally speaking, ICT systems are designed for the acquisition, storage, manipulation, transmission, retrieval and use of information. A successful implementation of an ICTS depends not only on the corresponding components like software, hardware and devices but it must also be able to cope with the overall architecture and its environment. Ideally speaking, ICTS support people in their business processes and in solving and supporting daily tasks and activities. They improve effectiveness, efficiency and reliability of enterprise business at the strategic, tactical and operational layers. The value of ICT and ICT systems engineering (cf. to (McGraw-Hill 2002))

> "... does indeed enable better designs of systems and existing organisations, it also enables the design of fundamentally new organisations and systems such as virtual corporations. Thus, efforts in this area include not only interactivity in working with clients to satisfy present needs but also awareness of future technological, organisational, and human concerns so as to support transition over time to new information technology-based services."

Typical ICTS today are applied in all the different industries we know, for example, automotive, avionics, manufacturing, entertainment and health care but also by the software industry itself. The systems range from administration and marketing systems to doctor's surgery information systems to manage patient records, trading systems for stock exchange, retail banking systems and many more. Let us take a closer look at retail banking as an example.

Fig. 1.4 Mobile banking, ATM, and bank counters

Today financial transactions are offered by a bank through a variety of different access channels like mobile banking using Smartphones and tablets, home banking using tablets and PCs, and Automated Teller Machines (also known as cashpoint). But the traditional bank counter is also available within the bank branch. Such a system as a whole has a complex infrastructure consisting of hardware, networks and devices (cf. Fig. 1.4). Software is running on the mentioned components, some visible to the banking customer and some running in the background. Sometimes such systems or subsystems run in real-time, at other times they run asynchronously or offline. The internet is also used to serve the customer's needs. For all these systems and subsystems, security and performance are mandatory characteristics.

A bank customer, for example, will use such a system to manage his bank account. He may need money in cash from the bank or want to transfer money from his account to another account, or want information about the current status of his own account. If an ATM fails to deliver its service there is usually another ATM nearby and the bank customer can go there. A similar situation may arise when the bank customer goes to "his" financial service clerk in a bank office. If the clerk "fails to deliver his service" there will be another clerk who will serve the customer. With online banking it is more difficult. Getting cash is not possible—at least not until we are allowed to print the banknotes ourselves. The remaining use cases can also be performed through online banking. In this case, it is important that the system only present the customer with his own information and transfers money only from the customer's account.

But what happens if there is an internet outage during the customer's transactions? In the best case, the system shuts down until the service can be offered again. In the worst case we do not know what the system is currently doing. But in all cases we need to be sure that nothing happens with our account or with information stored about us. Quality is a must and we have to ensure this before the system goes into production. What is the preferred quality of service for a bank customer? Can we allow, for example, online banking to have a lower quality level than cashpoint banking or a banking service by a clerk? What are the differences between the access channels? Historically, the clerk version has been the only way to perform all the use cases. He has to authorise access to the customer's account, he has to give the money to the customer, and he has to ensure that the electronic account is changed correctly after the withdrawal. The two other channels depend only on the correct functioning of the corresponding hardware and software. The ICT system authorises the customer based on predefined mechanisms. The

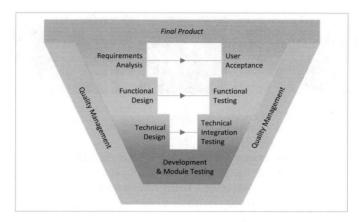

Fig. 1.5 V-Model in ICT world

cashpoint system either makes the transfer or provides the information, or pays out the money in cash. So the system is taking decisions instead of the former clerk, without knowing the customer it is serving.

How do we build systems like the above retail banking system today? How can we ascertain that everything has been done to reach the right level of quality? Usually we have two streams of quality assurance; testing as part of the development model, and quality management accompanying the development process. An example of such a development process in ICT is the V-Model XT (V-Modell XT 2004), which we have depicted in Fig. 1.5. For our purposes here, we do not need to differentiate between development paradigms, such as Agile or waterfall or incremental, as we are interested in a holistic enterprise ICT quality where the development models are part of the operational layer. Based on the development model above, let us turn to some aspects of an ICT project that was successfully completed in 2012 (cf. Table 1.1). The project processes are described using the scheme of Fig. 1.5.

The project started with the identification of ICT management's needs:

• Reduce maintenance costs in the future; and
• Increase efficiency through modern standard software.

Scoping and planning of the project resulted in:

• Replacement of the existing software for the management of bank accounts as part of an application cluster by standard software in the market;
• Integration of new software into various business processes at enterprise level;
• Definition of delta specifications of the business process models as extracts covering the new system; and
• Planning of various test stages and bug-fixing loops to ensure the quality of the new system.

Table 1.1 ICTS project outline

Outline of an ICT Project in the Financial Sector	
Requirements Analysis	
• no documentation of existing BP available	
• gap analysis between existing BP and functionality of the standard software	
• delta specification of additional requirements	
Functional Design	
• refinement of the BP to system processes	
• refinement business requirements by system requirements	
Technical Design	
• test environment management	
• separate test environments for unit and integration testing, system testing, system integration testing, user acceptance testing, migration testing	
• anonymised and migrated test data	
• an on-demand reset mechanism was not provided	
• test data management was solved internally by organisational means within the test team	
Development & Module Testing	
• customisation of the standard software	
• add-on development, and	**Quality Management:**
• module testing	
had been performed based on technical design	• reviews for all artefacts
Technical Integration Testing	
• unit and integration testing; *scope*: developers testing against detailed test design	
• peer-to-peer integration testing; *scope*: testing of interfaces between systems against system requirements	
• data migration testing (software and data); *scope*: testing of data migration system	
• performance testing data migration; *scope*: testing one-time data migration	
• BP performance testing; *scope*: testing selected business processes against business requirements	
• system integration testing; *scope*: testing new system use cases and their integration limited to business domains and system cluster	
Functional Testing	
• full end-to-end BP testing; *scope*: testing against real business	
• system testing; *scope*: functional testing of customising and new features against system requirements by developers; also individual front-end system	
User Acceptance	
• user acceptance testing; *scope*: covered by full-end-to-end testing	
• operational acceptance testing; *scope*: testing against technical requirements given by operations	

Quality management was installed throughout project execution. The quality of the corresponding artefacts in the process was ensured through reviews but no systematic and complete methodology was installed from the beginning until go-live. After user acceptance of the new ICT system, a so-called "dress rehearsal" took place before going live into the productive system environment.

From a quality perspective, the project had a sequence of testing stages to verify characteristics like functionality, performance, interoperability and data migration. Static characteristics and quality gates in early phases were not considered.

After completion of the project an evaluation of the test process was performed by the test team. There was some uncertainty about necessary coverage for the test basis, which was not fully documented or supported by corresponding specialists. During testing the test team also observed some hidden targets coming from different stakeholders. After go-live, product quality during the first 4 weeks as well as after the next few months was evaluated. The results were excellent: no severe errors occurred and daily business had not been disrupted.

In conclusion, the management of the company stated that testing involved too much effort and could be reduced for subsequent projects. Is management really asking for less effort and, therefore, less cost next time? How to specify operational quality requirements that also conform to Strategic quality requirements? How to balance quality requirements with budget and time? How is quality measured? How can we say that the delivered quality is the expected one?

Looking at the "magic triangle" from the project management perspective, we know that time-to-market and budgets seem easier to handle. Immediately after the end of the project we know whether the project was completed on time or not, and we also know whether the budget was overrun or not. But in terms of quality, when do we know whether the right level of quality has been achieved?

Embedded Systems Today

Generally speaking, embedded systems are designed to perform some specific tasks rather than being a general-purpose computer system for multiple tasks. The challenge in the ES world is the fact that the focus is not only on digital computing, as is the case in the ICT world, but also on an intelligent interplay between mechanical systems, electronic systems, computer systems and control systems. Sensors measure analogue signals from their environment, transform them into digital signals, combine them with signals from other sources, perform digital computation and trigger the corresponding actuators to conduct the intended tasks. Real-time constraints, as well as safety and robustness properties, must be continuously monitored and managed during the life of the embedded system and its components. Predictability of the embedded system's behaviour and its components is a key factor.

Typical embedded systems today are applied in most of the industries we know: e.g. automotive, avionics, manufacturing, entertainment, health care but also logistics and banking. Embedded systems range from complete cars, trains and planes to telecommunication systems, different kinds of industrial plants and many more. Car components, like control units for the anti-lock braking system or flight control systems, are also part of this world. Let us take a closer look at the control units of a particular car series as an example.

Fig. 1.6 Electronic control in the Mercedes E-series

The Mercedes E-series is a good example (cf. Fig. 1.6 and also (Thurner 2001)). Almost all functions of E-series are supported by electronic systems, for example:

- Powertrain;
- Comfort;
- Display systems;
- Telematics;
- Active and passive safety;
- Diagnosis; and
- Anti-theft.

The technical constraints of such systems, at low cost of course, are:

- Limited memory;
- Small CPU performance;
- Simple operating system;
- Static and fixed at compile-time;
- Hard real-time; and
- Networked Electronic Control Units like LIN, CAN and FlexRay.

Today, the radio and navigation system alone in the current Mercedes-Benz S-series requires over 20 million lines of code and contains nearly as many ECUs as the new Airbus A380 (excluding the plane's in-flight entertainment system). In total, this amounts to dozens of microprocessors running 100 million lines of code to get a premium car out of the driveway, "and this software is only going to get more complex" (Charette 2009).

Although software is one part of the various components of the whole system, it is in fact not the most important one. The interaction between all components is central. Because of the complexity of each component, it is common for specialised companies to be contracted to supply final integration of the whole system. The vertical integration of the integrating company itself is not as high as in the ICT world. This results in a multi-dimensional networked supply chain, where every participating partner has to ensure the component's quality needed for the whole system.

How do we build systems like a car? How can we ensure that everything is done to reach the right level of quality? In the embedded world it is usual to have at least

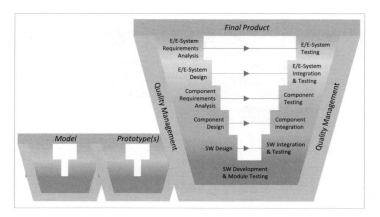

Fig. 1.7 Triple V-Model in the ES world

a "triple V" (cf. ISO 26262 2009), one for the modelling phase, another for the prototype(s) phase, and a third for the final product (cf. Fig. 1.7).

As part of all three development phases we again have two streams of quality assurance; validation and verification (testing) as part of the development process, and quality management, accompanying the development process. Again, for our purposes, we do not need other paradigms because we are interested in a holistic enterprise ICT quality, where the development models are part of the operational level. Taking the development model above, let us discuss some aspects of an ES project that is still running at the time of writing (cf. Table 1.2). The project processes are described using the scheme of Fig. 1.7. The project started with the identification of product management's needs:

- Reduce development and maintenance costs;
- Reduce exhaust emission to meet given standards;
- Increase safety; and
- Increase comfort.

Quality management was installed throughout project execution. The quality of the corresponding artefacts in the process was ensured through reviews, but no systematic and complete methodology was installed end-to-end.

Typical impacts of an embedded system's malfunctioning are threats to

- Life or physical condition;
- Financial conditions; and
- Quality issues.

This leads to a strong demand for error avoidance and early error detection. As presented in the project outline above, it is mandatory that quality management accompanies all project processes and activities in the embedded systems world. The goal is always to ensure, for all supplier chains, a minimum level of maturity in the relevant processes, products and components. Continuous control is necessary

Table 1.2 ES project outline

	Outline of an E/E Product Development Project in the Automotive Sector	
Model T Prototype(s) / Final Product	**E/E System – Requirements Analysis & Design** ● review of functional specifications ● conformity check safety	**Quality Management:** ● assessments for all suppliers
	Components – Requirements Analysis & Design ● review of functional specifications ● conformity check safety	● development health check (suppliers) ● compliance check and support for quality requirements, project management, development processes, test processes and quality of acceptance (OEM, suppliers)
	Software – Design ● evaluation of technical design ● conformity check safety	● support change management, configuration management, requirements management (OEM and suppliers)
	Software – Integration & Testing performed by OEM and suppliers	● planning and reporting on quality assurance results (statistics, KPIs)
	Components – Integration & Testing performed by OEM and suppliers	● review of standards for development
	E/E System – Integration & Testing (HiL, Breadboard Assemblies, Prototype Car, Car) performed by OEM and suppliers	● continuous evaluation of the maturity of processes and projects for critical ECUs

to maximise transparency and comparability to avoid unexpected results. What is correct from the start does not have to be corrected later on. This is the only way complex embedded systems, where many technical disciplines participate in development, can be integrated to build a complete system that behaves correctly and is affordable. Nevertheless, also in this embedded world, quality assurance coordinated and balanced along the supply chain is not yet a reality. A lot can still be improved (Anders et al 2013).

The Value of ICTS Quality Today

The value of ICT systems quality is aligning ICT with business demands in the right way. Quality, by its nature, is multi-dimensional and always a sequence of compromises. Quality is composed of many different characteristics, which are not always independent of each other. Moreover, one characteristic can have a negative or positive influence on another characteristic.

Tom DeMarco (DeMarco 2001) says that "the quality of a software product is in first instance a function of its usefulness". As an example, he discusses photo shop software which has a lot of useful functions for photo editing, like making compositions from basic pictures: "take part of a picture where my wife looks pretty good and I myself look angry and combine this with a part of another picture where I am looking friendly and my wife is not present". Even knowing that this software sometimes leads to crashes and other problems, we pay for it and use it because of its "usefulness" in most of the cases. But, how do we define the usefulness of a system or software product and how can we measure it? How do we know the usefulness unless we have applied the software? Or is it simply the number of users or the price?

Sometimes, quality of a system or software product is defined through the functionality and the technical properties when it is released. Some of the characteristics are measurable, like "the reaction time of a program on a request is expected to be within 10 s", whereas others like "the colour of controls on a screen must be usable" are more individual. Sometimes good quality for one person is low quality for another person. For example, we did some exercises with students participating in a lecture called "Healthcare Management—Information Management" at the University of Applied Sciences in Cologne. We showed them a few homepages of various German health insurance companies and asked them to describe the quality of these pages from their personal perspectives. The results were extremely divergent with respect to, for example, position and colour of controls, useful search items, provided functions, performance indications and other topics. This demonstrates that a kind of individual weighting will be applied on functionality as well as technical properties.

A similar picture can be drawn from our experiences of more than 7,000 quality assurance and testing projects from the private and the public sector. Stakeholders have different views and expectations of the quality of ICTS. If a user does not get the right quality he has to live with limitations which might lead to inefficient workflows and unwanted costs. Therefore, the business owner for the system has to define characteristics of right quality and agree on them with all other relevant stakeholders. The business owner has to decide not only on the functional and other requirements for the system but also all other quality characteristics needed for an efficient support of daily business operations. And they have to provide budgets. Furthermore, there are architects and developers who have to design and implement the corresponding product from the requirements. They have to ensure all required characteristics when using the system, but they also have to ensure all required characteristics for operating the system. However, we know that in projects, as well as in organisations, there are conflicting objectives between different participants and stakeholders that cause a multitude of deficiencies.

Because people are always interested in improving—higher, faster, longer—it is given that the quality of a system or software product is not fixed over time. A product characteristic that is important for a stakeholder at the beginning of the system's lifecycle might be dispensable after a certain amount of time because the stakeholder has changed expectations. In this sense we could perhaps speak of "aging system quality" (cf. Chap. 2).

Quality is a notion which is not easy to define like, for example, budget and time. When we talk about budget we usually refer to a specific number and the same is true for time, which we express as a certain date or amount of days. That makes the definition of quality even more difficult and leads to workarounds such as "good quality is delivered when all test cases are executed and no serious errors occur at the end". Does this really give an accurate indication of the quality of the system? Obviously it does not because we do not know the quality of the test cases. We can certainly follow this reasoning and try to find out the quality of the test cases and so on.

The notion of process quality came into existence some years ago. Standards like ISO 9001 (2008) and ISO 15504 (2011) or CMMI (Chrissis et al. 2011) provide suitable process and assessment models, which can be applied in a constructive as well as an analytical manner. In the very beginning of such process models, it was expected that quality could be "guaranteed" by "only" performing a good process, as the resulting product would also be good. This was a great misunderstanding or misjudgement. Of course good processes also tend to result in better quality of their results, but there is no inevitability. There are a lot of influencing factors and dependencies between these factors that determine the results. For the purpose of our discussion we can change the question of "good" quality to "good" processes for a specific project. We know that having a good process in place does not necessarily lead to artefacts and products that fulfil the needs of the stakeholders. On the contrary, we know that bad processes could (in theory) also produce good products; but the probability is low. We also know that many of these deficiencies are due to needs that are not clearly described, or not at all, or we leave out considerations about the context and environment in which the system or software product has to perform.

What are the reasons for such situations? Logically speaking, having a good process in place is necessary but not sufficient. This means that if a good process is in place the probability of getting high quality products is much higher than if there is no good process. Nevertheless, a good process has to be balanced with required quality, budget, time, knowledge and documentation of real needs, available human resources (qualifications, background knowledge and motivation), technical resources (techniques, tools, test environments), etc. The same process can be good for one organisation but less effective for another. Also, in this case excellent people in organisations and companies can ensure that impending deficiencies will not have too much impact on business and daily life. If quality of a system or software product is as volatile as described, we need better strategies, concepts and frameworks that maximise transparency about quality and risk.

What Can We Learn from Today's ICT and Embedded Systems Worlds?

ICT and embedded systems have some important similarities but also some differences. A number of characteristics have become obvious from the discussions above. We have chosen ten important categories, depicted in Table 1.3.

The category "Quality requirements" contains a set of values—low, medium, high—which should give an indication of what, in our experience, the importance of the corresponding quality characteristic is, e.g. if safety is regarded as "low" in

Table 1.3 Comparison of ICTS and ES

Categories	World of ICT Systems	World of Embedded Systems
Environment & Communication	diverse channels with different devices and other systems in the environment; embedded in a complex environment → dynamically changing environments	sensors, actuators and other systems in the environment; embedded in an electronic and/or electromechanical environment → static environments
Systemic View	focus on software and applications; no systemic thinking	focus on products, product lines, generations of products; significant systemic thinking
Variants	increasing demands for standard software due to increasing number of platforms	huge number of variants due to different models, options and country-specific rules
Lifetime	dependent on the type of system/application ranging from several months to more than 10 years with several releases; not taken into account during development	from an individual product perspective less than 10 years; from a product company perspective, 20 years and more (including development and production until disposal)
Quality Requirements	dependent on the type of system/application	mostly independent of the type of system
—Selected Samples— *Functional Correctness*	high	high
Time Criticality	medium	high
Safety	low	high
Reliability	low	high
Availability	high	high
Security	medium	high
Maintainability	Medium	high
Quality Management and Quality Assurance	quality is poorly integrated into the application/software lifecycle; quality is considered mostly in terms of dynamic testing	quality is an integral part of the product lifecycle and strongly proven by quality management, validation and verification means
Impacts of Missing Quality	threats to financial conditions, business quality, enterprise image and perhaps even enterprise survival	threats to life and physical conditions, financial conditions, quality issues, enterprise survival
Distributed Development	becoming more relevant due to cost pressure	high distribution due to supply chain
Supply Chains	one or a few participants	many participants
Certification	sometimes in place, mainly optional	mandatory in many cases due to interoperability and safety and security requirements

the ICT world but "high" in the embedded world, it is from our experience with over 7,000 projects. From the Table 1.3 above we can summarise that

- The interaction between ICT systems and their environments seems to be less predefined than for embedded systems and, therefore, the behaviour of ICT systems seems to be less predictable;
- A systemic approach, as well as lifetime considerations, lead to more trustworthiness of embedded world products; this is less true in the ICT world;
- A lot of quality characteristics are key factors for products in the embedded world and many actions are taken to ensure quality; this is less true in the ICT world and most often it is individually defined for each project;
- Supply chains and distributed development are normal in the embedded world and provides flexible organisational structures, including outsourcing to specialised partners; this is less the case in ICT.

In conclusion, the whole procurement process in ICT, including development and subsequent operations and maintenance, focuses too much on the software part and not enough on how the whole system functions during its lifecycle as a product. The added value of quality management and quality engineering is much lower than it could be. The costs are much higher than they could be. A systemic approach for ICT systems is required and quality must become an integral part of the whole lifecycle. Quality is the bridge between business and ICT.

1.3 Why Industrialisation Matters for ICT Product Quality

Adam Smith outlined in his famous "Wealth of Nations" (cf. Sutherland 2008) that increase of productivity in a society is founded in specialisation and industrialism, essentially represented by the concept of division of labour. In Smith's work, the different approaches to manufacture pins were investigated and compared. The same principles can now be applied to the software industry and reflect the evolution seen over the past decades.

As the software industry has evolved over time, fundamental changes in business and the supporting ICT organisations have taken place. Recent years have seen the transition from integrated full-service units to specialisation of departments and companies along the various functions required to run business and their supporting ICT organisations. Additionally, cost efficiency puts added pressure on executives looking to focus on their core competencies and outsource non-core tasks to specialised providers. But how does one apply industrialisation concepts to an operational ICT organisation with well-established structures, processes and conventions? To systems that have been developed and maintained for 20 years or more and have experienced a large number of changes resulting in manifold maintenance activities?

Although industrialisation is best known and applied in the embedded world, it is still of low maturity in the ICT world. Following (Buxmann et al 2008), industrialisation is a "historically grown management concept which allows for cost-effective manufacturing of products". Starting points for Buxmann et al. are standardisation, specialisation and automation. From publications about industrialisation, such as (Buxmann et al 2008), (Capgemini 2012), (Simon et al 2014) or definitions in Wikipedia (Wiki-Industrie 2013) and (Wiki-Industrialisation 2013), we can infer that industrialisation is the process of

"... development and implementation of industrial production types."

Industrialisation as a process has impact on products and intermediate products, as well as on business processes of the corresponding industry. A key factor in this process is the technology and its evolution. There are a number of typical characteristics for industrial production that can be differentiated. In our view, some are

Table 1.4 Characteristics of industrial production

Typical Characteristics of Industrial Production / Manufacturing	Relevant for Software Industry
Mass Production	no
Mechanisation	partly
Automation	yes
High Technological Intensity	yes
Work Sharing	yes
Regular Production	yes
Separation of Production Site from Housing and Leisure	partly
Standardisation	yes
Exchangeability of Products or Components	yes
Production on Stock for an Anonymous Market	no

relevant for the software industry and some are not. For a brief overview refer to Table 1.4.

The products in the software industry are software and software-based systems, which are designed and implemented for taking over particular tasks and supporting certain activities along predefined business processes. The key processes in the software industry are development, implementation, operation and maintenance. All processes, as well as the products, are complex and costly and often the result is disappointing. For a long time it has been regarded more as an art than an engineering discipline that applies industrial production paradigms. The survey (Capgemini 2012) gives an overview of the allocation of ICT budgets today. Six different pillars are defined:

- 28.5 % for hardware, networks and infrastructure in general;
- 21.8 % for projects addressing major releases of existing software;
- 20.8 % for ongoing software maintenance and projects addressing minor releases;
- 13.7 % for projects for procurement, development and implementation of innovations;
- 8.0 % for projects addressing the evaluation of innovations; and
- 7.2 % buffer for unforeseen activities and projects.

These numbers show that 42.6 % of a company's entire ICT budget is spent on keeping existing software running and up-to-date due to failures and change requests. Therefore, looking for industrialised approaches in ICT and asking for affordable quality are valid concerns.

Professional activities in a software product lifecycle typically range from identification of needs, definition of scope and project planning, requirements analysis, functional and technical design, development, integration and testing, implementation, operations and maintenance, and disposal [cf. Fig. 1.8 as an example derived from the model published by the US Department of Justice (US Department of Justice 2003)]. The phases from start to implementation normally represent no more than 30 % of the effort spent on the product during its

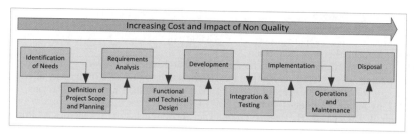

Fig. 1.8 A sample lifecycle model

whole lifecycle. Usually the phases from requirements analysis up to implementation are projects that are planned and initiated in the second phase. It is important to note that the later deficiencies and failures are found in a system, the higher the costs and the greater the impacts on the system, its environment and its quality properties.

We agree with Martyn Jeffries (cf. Fice 2013) that the whole product lifecycle can be made more effective and efficient if industrialisation is built in. By industrialisation we mean "the process of development and implementation of industrial production forms in a product (systems and software) lifecycle". Industrialisation often means standardisation, specialisation, and automation (cf. Buxmann et al 2008).

Three ways of defining industrialisation in the software industry can be derived from Fig. 1.8:

1. Industrialisation of the whole lifecycle;
2. Industrialisation of one box or a sequence of boxes; or
3. Industrialisation of two independent parallel streams as part of the whole lifecycle.

We propose to follow the last way. Ideally, industrialisation in the software industry should be split into two parallel tasks, namely development (in a narrow sense) and quality engineering. Therefore, we will discuss in detail our model of industrialisation in Chap. 5. This model is different from the definitions already presented above and used in publications like (BITKOM 2010) and (Capgemini 2012). How this will lead to affordable quality will be discussed in Chap. 7.

References and Links

Anders R, Bölter P, Thurner T (2013) Industrialised test automation—harmonising testing for mechatronic systems. In: Vos D, Ericsson I, Brunnstein J, Euteneuer S (eds) Whitepaper book—thought leadership 2013. SQS, Cologne

BITKOM (ed) (2010) Industrielle Softwareentwicklung, Leitfaden und Orientierungshilfe. BITKOM, Berlin

Boland T (2010) Toward a preliminary framework for assessing the trustworthiness of software. NIST, Gaithersburg

BSI (2006) Pervasive computing: Entwicklungen und Auswirkungen. Bundesamt für Sicherheit in der Informationstechnik. BSI, Bonn

Butler J (2012) A History of information technology and systems. University of Arizona. http://www.tcf.ua.edu/AZ/ITHistoryOutline.htm. Retrieved 2 August 2012 (Originally developed as a lecture for MAR 203 Concepts in New Media, a course at the University of Arizona, summer 1997, by Jeremy G. Butler.)

Buxmann P, Diefenbach H, Hess T (2008) Die Softwareindustrie: Ökonomische Prinzipien, Strategien, Perspektiven. Springer, Berlin

Capgemini (2012) Studie IT-Trends 2012—Business-IT-Alignment sichert die Zukunft. Capgemini, Berlin

Charette R (2009) This car runs on code. http://spectrum.ieee.org/green-tech/advanced-cars/this-car-runs-on-code. Posted 1 Feb 2009, 5:00 GMT. Retrieved 7 Nov 2013

Chrissis M, Konrad M, Shrum S (2011) CMMI for development: guidelines for process integration and product improvement, 3rd edn. Pearson Education, Boston

Dargie W, Poellabauer C (2010) Fundamentals of wireless sensor networks—theory and practice. Wiley, Chichester

DeMarco T (2001) Spielräume—Projektmanagement jenseits von Burn-out, Stress und Effizienzwahn. Carl Hanser, München

Fice S (2013) Industrialisation of IT quality to be the norm by 2018. http://www.manufacturingdigital.com/innovators/industrialisation-of-it-quality-to-be-the-norm-by-2018. Retrieved 13 Nov 2013

Gibb F (2012) Gambler loses to computer virus. http://www.thetimes.co.uk/tto/law/article3447502.ece. Retrieved 12 Nov 2013

GSMA (2012) Experience a world where everything intelligently connects: The Connected Life. http://connectedlife.gsma.com/wp-content/uploads/2012/02/conn_lif_pospaper_web_01_11-13.pdf. Retrieved 7 Nov 2013

ISO 15504 (2011) Information technology—process assessment, ISO/IEC 15504. International Organization for Standardization (ISO), Geneva

ISO 26262 (2009) Road vehicles—functional safety, ISO/DIS 26262. International Organization for Standardization (ISO), Geneva

ISO 9001 (2008) Qualitätsmanagementsysteme—Anforderungen, ISO 9001:2008. International Organization for Standardization (ISO), Geneva

Lever R (2012) Vote glitch reports pile up in US election (Update). http://phys.org/news/2012-11-vote-glitch-pile-election.html. Retrieved 12 Nov 2012

Linsky K (2012) United Airlines software glitch strands travelers again. http://www.pcworld.com/article/2014282/united-airlines-software-glitch-strands-travelers-again.html. Retrieved 12 Nov 2013

Mattern F (2008) Allgegenwärtige Datenverarbeitung—Trends, Visionen, Auswirkungen. In: Rossnagel A et al (eds) Digitale Visionen—Zur Gestaltung allgegenwärtiger Informationstechnologien. Springer, Berlin

McGraw-Hill (2002) McGraw-Hill Concise Encyclopedia of Engineering—Information Technology. http://encyclopedia2.thefreedictionary.com/Information+technology+systems. Retrieved 20 Nov 2013

Mellis W (2001) Process and product orientation in software development and their effect on software quality management. In: Wieczorek M, Meyerhoff D (eds) Software quality, state of the art in management, testing, and tools. Springer, Berlin

NHTSA (2012) BMW recalling 7 series for software problems. http://latest-cars-updates.blogspot.de/2012/10/bmw-recalling-7-series-for-software.html. Retrieved 30 Oct 2013

Russolillo S (2012) NYSE to cancel trades in six stocks after trading problems. Wall Street Journal Blogs, MarketBeat. http://blogs.wsj.com/marketbeat/2012/08/01/nyse-to-cancel-trades-in-six-stocks-after-trading-snafu/. Posted 1 Aug 2012–3:39 PM. Retrieved 30 Oct 2013

Simon F, Koßmann A, Kuhrmann M, Méndez Fernández D (2014) Wunsch oder Wirklichkeit? Professionelle Softwareentwicklung "Made in Germany". http://www.sigs-datacom.de/fachzeitschriften/objektspektrum/aktuelle-ausgabe.html. Retrieved 10 Jan 2014

Sutherland K (ed) (2008) An inquiry into the nature and causes of the wealth of nations. Oxford University Press, New York

Thurner (2001) Software aspects of EE-systems integration. Presentation at 1st international symposium on automotive control. Shanghai

US Department of Justice (2003) Information Resources Management—The Department of Justice Systems Development Life Cycle Guidance Document. http://www.justice.gov/jmd/irm/lifecycle/table.htm. Retrieved 13 Nov 2013

V-Modell XT (2004) V-Modell XT, Teil 2: Eine Tour durch das V-Modell. Bundesrepublik Deutschland. ftp://ftp.tu-clausthal.de/pub/institute/informatik/v-modell-xt/Releases/1.2/Dokumentation/pdf/V-Modell-XT-Teil2.pdf. Retrieved 20 Nov 2013

Webb T (2012) E.ON comes clean and pays the penalty. http://www.thetimes.co.uk/tto/business/industries/utilities/article3613509.ece. Posted 28 Nov 2012—12:01 AM. Retrieved 12 Nov 2012

Weiser M (1991) The computer for the 21st century. Sci Am 265 (3). http://wiki.daimi.au.dk/pca/_files/weiser-orig.pdf. Retrieved 20 Nov 2013

Wiki-Industrie (2013). http://de.wikipedia.org/wiki/Industrie. Retrieved 20 Nov 2013

Wiki-Industrialisation (2013) http://en.wikipedia.org/wiki/Industrialisation. Retrieved 20 Nov 2013

Zappone C (2012) Leap year blamed for HICAPS stumble. http://www.theage.com.au/business/leap-year-blamed-for-hicaps-stumble-20120229-1u1z7.html. Retrieved 12 Nov 2012

http://commons.wikimedia.org/wiki/File:Abacus_1_%28PSF%29.png?uselang=en. Retrieved 31 Oct 2013

http://commons.wikimedia.org/wiki/File:Arts_et_Metiers_Pascaline_dsc03869.jpg. Retrieved 11 Dec 2013

http://commons.wikimedia.org/wiki/File:Babbages_difference_engine_1832.jpg. Retrieved 11 Dec 2013

http://en.wikipedia.org/wiki/File:Ada_Lovelace.jpg. Retrieved 11 Dec 2013

http://www.weller.to/his/img/zuse_z1.jpg. Retrieved 11 Dec 2013

http://en.wikipedia.org/wiki/File:IBM_Blue_Gene_P_supercomputer.jpg. Retrieved 11 Dec 2013

http://www.weltdergadgets.de/wp-content/uploads/2012/01/Acer-Aspire-5750G-Laptop.jpg. Retrieved 11 Dec 2013 http://commons.wikimedia.org/wiki/File:IPAD_black.png?uselang=en. Retrieved 11 Dec 2013

 http://commons.wikimedia.org/wiki/File:IPhone_4_Mock_No_Shadow_PSD.png. Retrieved 11 Dec 2013

 http://www.solingen-internet.de/si-hgw/images/steinbeil.jpg. Retrieved 11 Dec 2013

 http://commons.wikimedia.org/wiki/File:Dampfma_gr.jpg. Retrieved 11 Dec 2013

 Esther M. Zimmer Lederberg. http://www.estherlederberg.com/EImages/Extracurricular/Cloth/FILE0173%20Cartwright%27s%202nd%20Power%20Loom.jpg. Retrieved 11 Dec 2013

 http://commons.wikimedia.org/wiki/File:PSM_V69_D434_Bell_centennial_single_pole_telephone.png. Retrieved 11 Dec 2013

 http://en.wikipedia.org/wiki/File:1885Benz.jpg. Retrieved 11 Dec 2013

 http://www.armedforces-int.com/upload/image_files/military-electronic-parts.jpg. Retrieved 11 Dec 2013

 Mercedes-Benz Classic

 http://www.mibar.net/Libraries/Images/Industry-Specific-Software-Solutions.sflb.ashx. Retrieved 11 Dec 2013

 http://www.srr.com/assets/Stock-Price-Performance.preview.gif. Retrieved 11 Dec 2013

 http://www.at.aero.de/content/pics/p_2281.jpg. Retrieved 11 Dec 2013

 http://seminartopics.info/wp-content/uploads/2012/03/pervasive-computing.jpg. Retrieved 11 Dec 2013

http://www.web3.ie/wp-content/uploads/2011/08/Global-Communication.jpg.
Retrieved 11 Dec 2013

 http://thoughtsfrombroadstreet.files.wordpress.com/2013/04/mobile-health-monitoring.jpg. Retrieved 11 Dec 2013

 http://ehplus.areavoices.com/2013/02/23/track-golden-eagle/. Retrieved 11 Dec
2013

 http://db.cger.nies.go.jp/gem/moni-e/moni/image/outline0512.jpg. Retrieved 11 Dec
2013

 http://www.zvei.org/SiteCollectionImages/Themen/Industrie-40/ir/474/0/Nationale-Roadma-Embedded-Systems.jpg. Retrieved 11 Dec 2013

 http://www.zvei.org/SiteCollectionImages/Themen/Industrie-40/ir/474/0/Nationale-Roadma-Embedded-Systems.jpg. Retrieved 11 Dec 2013

 http://dev.emcelettronica.com/rtos-embedded-systems. Retrieved 11 Dec 2013

 https://www.postbank.de/postbank/docs/219_799_pb_pr_pressebilder_direktvertrieb_tanverfahren_chipTAN_comfort_auf_dem_iPhone_n_5.jpg. Retrieved 11 Jan 2014

 http://2.bp.blogspot.com/_oBRbTQRZwVI/TQuDQNAYdYI/AAAAAAAAAeg/YDEDOlMY8w8/s320/atm.jpg. Retrieved 11 Dec 2013

 http://www.ohio.com/polopoly_fs/1.63196.1308489774!/remoteImage/httpImage/image.jpg_gen/derivatives/landscape_500/bank-02.jpg. Retrieved 11 Jan 2014

Chapter 2
The Four "P"s of Enterprise ICT

A holistic quality approach is founded on a certain view on enterprises and their ICT. Characterising enterprises and their ICT is a complex task and many disciplines and people have done excellent work on it. It is not our goal here to provide another theory of Business Administration, Computer Science, ICT Management or the like. But we do aim to present a holistic approach for quality issues that are vertically and horizontally aligned with the enterprise's organisation. Such an approach affects the people that work there, the implemented processes, the implemented ICT products and applications, and the defined ICT programmes and projects. We call this the four "P"s of enterprise ICT.

Before we discuss the four "P"s in subsequent sections we will shed some light on enterprises and their ICT. We will discuss enterprises as black boxes and depict the relevant objects of enterprise ICT. From this chapter on, we will focus only on the ICT world and discuss our concepts in the context of ICT systems and products.

2.1 Our View on Enterprise ICT

Business today is heavily dependent on ICT systems, which not only collect and provide data and information to their end users, but also play an increasingly active role in decision processes. Remember the example, for instance, where in August 2013 the NASDAQ fell into trouble because the trading software made decisions based on "a confluence of unprecedented events", as they claimed (Stafford 2013). What we would like to demonstrate with this example is not that ICT systems sometimes fail to deliver as expected but that those systems take decisions and actively initiate business processes with impacts at the expense of third parties. Sometimes these systems act together with humans and sometimes they act in isolation because the corresponding rules and instructions have been implemented in the system's software. In the latter case, we need to rely on the system's behaviour and need to ensure upfront that it is safe and reliable. As we know, it is not always easy to define precisely what correct behaviour is, but without the right

M. Wieczorek et al., *Systems and Software Quality*,
DOI 10.1007/978-3-642-39971-8_2, © Springer-Verlag Berlin Heidelberg 2014

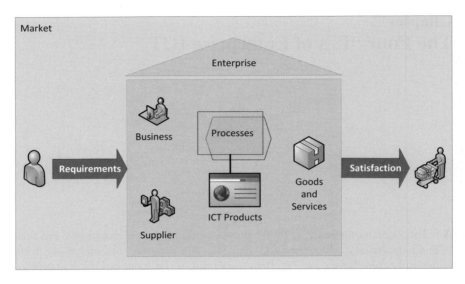

Fig. 2.1 An abstract view on enterprises

quality, it becomes a game of pure chance. This should not be a goal to which enterprises and their leaders aspire.

Let us start our construction of a holistic enterprise ICT quality approach with a small illustration characterising an enterprise in its market. In our systemic view, an enterprise can be regarded as a black box, located within markets and getting requirements from their markets, customers, and potential customers and being able to satisfy their customers' needs. Looking into this black box, it is usually driven by experienced and intelligent people using powerful ICT products to efficiently conduct the corresponding processes for building and offering the enterprise's products, i.e. goods and/or services. It is a view that Richard Barrett calls a "machine with a mind" (cf. Barrett 1998). This is schematically depicted in Fig. 2.1.

There are people who work in management, administration, business domains and ICT. They are permanent staff, external consultants or suppliers. They are recruited or assigned at some point in time best suited for the appointed position. Processes mostly break down into business processes, management processes, ICT processes and project processes. Processes provide a proven systematic way of performing various tasks in the respective domain of an enterprise. A process is defined through its goals, preconditions, inputs, outputs, sequence of activities together with the intermediate artefacts and final products and also employs methods and tools. Powerful ICT products or parts of these products are important resources for people to perform their business processes efficiently. Last but not least we have the business products to be offered and sold to customers. The business products are goods or services or combinations of both. Projects are started as an organisational structure with fixed targets, like building new products or maintaining existing ones, and are limited in time and budget.

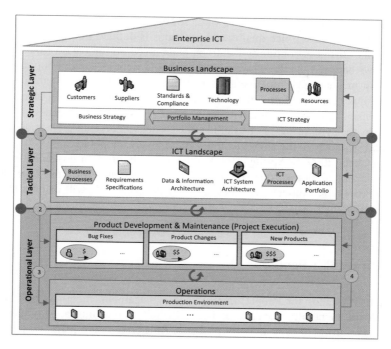

Fig. 2.2 Enterprise ICT

Of course, quality of ICT products is always presupposed and sometimes ICT quality is actually in place. The question frequently is, to what degree? Looking at an enterprise in more detail, three organisational layers can be distinguished: the strategic, the tactical and the operational layer. To align ICT with business demands it is necessary that ICT as a whole and ICT quality in particular are represented at all three layers. Following the ideas of information management and information engineering (cf. for example Hares 1992; Heinrich and Lehner 2005; and Krcmar 2005) our view on enterprise ICT is depicted in Fig. 2.2.

Enterprise ICT and its quality is a strategic, tactical and operational topic. On a strategic layer we have the business landscape of the enterprise, comprising the strategies for business and ICT, standards and compliance with external laws and regulations, such as Basel III and SEPA, national and international ICT-related standards, trends in technologies for effective and efficient enterprise ICT and the business processes of the enterprise. This is also the layer where responsibility for governance lies (see Chap. 4). This list is not exhaustive, but it gives a good summary for our purposes. The next layer, i.e. the tactical one, consists of the ICT landscape comprising all the ICT products (ICT systems). It is the layer where the implementation of the ICT strategies, planning, monitoring and control of ICT infrastructure and ICT projects is done. For the next and lowest layer we make a distinction between product development and maintenance (projects) on the one hand and operations on the other hand. Typically, operations comprise the running of ICT products, including all hardware, software, infrastructure and user (customer) support. The service quality of operations is defined through service layer agreements. Business continuity has to be guaranteed on the basis of these SLAs. The arrows between the three layers on the left and right side define top-down and bottom-up mechanisms implementing a feedback loop to ensure that the targets from the upper layer are fulfilled by the lower layers and that the lower layers report on fulfilment. There is another iterative process in place between two layers, denoted by the symbol "↺". For example, the strategy of an enterprise is developed in several steps where the strategic and tactical layers cooperate.

As in Chen (2009) or Spring (1992), although with different goals and interpretations, the foundation of our enterprise ICT model is given by the four "P"s of People, Processes, Products, and Projects and Portfolio. We will discuss them in more detail further on.

2.2 First "P": People

The first "P" stands for People, in this case management, members of staff and stakeholders. Generally speaking it is the "who" of reaching a particular goal. People have different roles in daily business. Roles like board member, executive manager, product owner, project manager and project member, team leader and team member are defined within an enterprise. All people are internally driven by their own values and beliefs and externally noticed by their actions and behaviours (cf. Barrett 2006). In this sense, they form a human system as part of an enterprise and constitute the "mind of the machine" as referred to above. The success of an enterprise strongly depends on an efficient interplay between all the four "P"s. Therefore, it is important to know people's motivation and goals, and not only to measure, monitor and improve their actions and behaviours.

Internal to the enterprise, know-how and experience of management and staff members is as important as profound knowledge about the stakeholders' views and interests. Because of cost requirements the number of adequate people for the different roles is mostly limited. Take a simple example with great impact from the auditing field:

> Due to a warning resulting from an external audit, an enterprise had to show what it had done to ensure quality of the central accounting system. Because of missing test and quality reports the enterprise defined a project to establish quality assurance in the form of a so-called test case portfolio for every ICT system. To build the portfolios, key users from the business departments had to be involved. But as is most often the case a key user—as the name indicates—has more than one task. Other people with adequate know-how were not available and so the project was delayed.

Is this normal business practice which we simply have to accept or can we eliminate such situations through preventive actions? What are the options we have? From our viewpoint, qualifying more people in the same topics to relieve the key users in any situation is one option; getting experienced people from outside

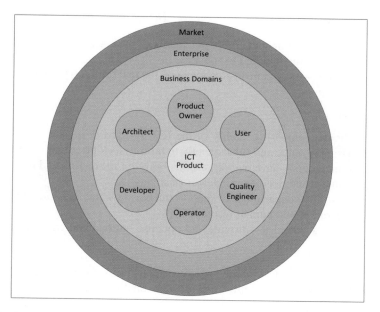

Fig. 2.3 Enterprise staff and stakeholders

the enterprise is a second option; and making the processes more productive is a third option. The latter then directly leads to questions like "what is the enterprise's core competency", "is it possible to outsource all non-core tasks", and "what are the preconditions for such transformations". For process concerns we refer to the Process "P" below. From the people's perspective, organisational change and transformation is always a question of aligning the people's interests with the interests of the enterprise. Therefore, we will look at different stakeholders of ICT products.

Different stakeholders have different views and expectations on correctly functioning ICT, which are applied in alignment with the business demands and which support daily business process execution. Also, their view on the quality of such ICT systems is determined by individual requirements and may change over time. Relevant stakeholders are first of all customers and market competitors. At enterprise level we have shareholders, board members and business domains. When going into more detail and looking especially into product development and maintenance, as well as operations, we have stakeholders like the internal user, the product owner, the quality engineer, the business and system architects, the developer and last but not least the operator in the production centre. They all have their roles in the enterprise, as depicted schematically in Fig. 2.3. The question that remains is what are the stakeholders' views and expectations on quality of the ICT systems in use?

What are the stakeholders' requirements for quality and what happens if the required quality is missing?

1. Market

   - Customers—require and accept the quality of the corresponding products and the quality of the buying channels;
   - Competitors—may gain an advantage on the market if the product or channel quality is poor.

2. Enterprise

   - Shareholders—missing quality of the ICT systems or channels may lead to decreasing revenue and subsequently to falling stock price and loss of money;
   - Board members—have overall responsibility for the quality and reputation of the business and decide on investment in quality;
   - Administrative departments—support the business and ICT, such as financial administration and human resources;
   - Enterprise academies—provide and organise internal and external seminars.

3. Business domains

   - (Business domain) Managers—have responsibility for the requirements for the ICT systems, including the detailed quality characteristics, and must accept ICT quality afterwards;
   - Key users—need quality for their daily work and therefore define requirements, including the detailed quality characteristics, and verify the quality during acceptance.

4. Product-related

   - Product Owner—is responsible for a product and its quality;
   - (Internal) End users—are affected in their daily work by missing quality and are interested in achieving stable and reliable systems with good performance and security;
   - Quality engineer—refines high-level quality characteristics down to design and code level and validates and verifies them to find out where the errors and causes lie before the system goes live;
   - Architect—refines requirements to design level as technical specifications for the developer;
   - Developer—implements the systems or changes with a certain quality using the functional and technical specifications;
   - Operator—has responsibility for operating all systems in the enterprise's ICT landscape and is therefore responsible for business continuity if missing quality leads to business disruption.

One question remains: who is responsible for the whole ICT systems landscape? Have we forgotten a key stakeholder? Or are they included in one of the above-mentioned roles? Or is this mostly not defined? We believe that the overall responsibility for ICT strategy and ICT landscape is given to the CIO or ICT Director at board level.

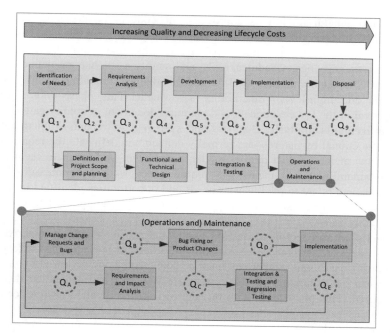

Fig. 2.4 Product lifecycle model

2.3 Second "P": Processes

The second "P" stands for Processes, which constitute the relationship between technology, methodology and people. Generally speaking it is the "how" of reaching a particular goal. Enterprise processes can be broken down into business processes, management processes, ICT processes and project processes. In the first instance, we are interested in processes in a product lifecycle. Our preferred model is presented in Fig. 2.4. It is a closed box that has a starting point, where product needs evolve, and a terminal point, where that same product is taken out of operation. The lifecycle is amended by so-called quality gates after each phase. Let us briefly discuss the basic model, encompassing nine phases, where "operations and maintenance" is again subdivided into five further phases. The phases are similar to the lifecycle model in (US Department of Justice 2003) but not identical and are complemented by quality gates. Note that all phases require more or less interaction between business and ICT.

1. **Identification of needs**: This phase starts when a business need or opportunity is identified. The needs and opportunities are documented in a concept proposal. This phase ends with the approval of the concept proposal in quality gate Q_1.
2. **Definition of scope and project planning**: Feasibility and appropriateness of the concept proposal are reviewed, the scope of the planned system is identified

and the general funding is approved. The concept is further developed to describe impacts on the business, staff and costumer privacy. To ensure the systems provide the required capability on-time and within budget, project resources, activities, schedules, tools; and quality assurance are defined. Additionally, a suitable product quality model is defined, including security certification and high-level vulnerability assessment. This phase ends with the approval of the system concept and planning document in quality gate Q_2.

3. **Requirements analysis**: Business and system requirements—functional and non-functional by nature—are formally defined and delineate the requirements in terms of the product quality model; e.g. system performance, security and maintainability requirements. All requirements need to be measurable and testable and relate to the business needs and opportunities identified in the first phase. This phase ends with the approval of the detailed requirements document in quality gate Q_3.

4. **Functional and technical design**: Functional and technical characteristics of the system are designed, the operating environment is established, everything requiring user input or approval must be documented and reviewed by the user, physical characteristics of the system are specified and a detailed design is prepared. This phase ends with the approval of the detailed design document in quality gate Q_4.

5. **Development**: The detailed specifications of the design document are translated into hardware, communications, and executable software. The software must be unit tested, integrated, and retested in a systematic manner to conform to the product quality model. Hardware is assembled and tested to conform to the product quality model. This phase ends with the approval of the detailed test completion report in quality gate Q_5.

6. **Integration and testing**: The various components of the system are integrated and systematically tested to conform to the product quality model. Here, functional as well as non-functional requirements have to be satisfied. Prior to installing and operating the system in a production environment, the system must undergo certification and accreditation, if necessary. This phase ends with the approval of the detailed integration and test completion report in quality gate Q_6.

7. **Implementation**: The system is installed and made operational in the production environment. This phase continues until the system landscape is operating in production in accordance with the defined requirements. This phase ends with the statement of acceptance approved by the Operations department in quality gate Q_7.

8. **Operations and maintenance**: This phase breaks down logically into two different activity clusters; system operation, which is an ongoing task ending with the disposal of the system in the last phase, and system maintenance, which is a task performed each time a corresponding request appears. In the Operations department, the system is monitored for continued performance in accordance with user requirements, and necessary system modifications are incorporated. The operational system is periodically assessed through In-Process Reviews to

determine how it can be made more efficient and effective. Operations continue as long as the system landscape can be effectively adapted to respond to an organisation's needs. When modifications or changes are identified, the following sub-phases are entered. This phase ends with the end of system operation in quality gate Q_8;

(a) **Manage change requests and bugs**: Similar to phases 1, 2 and 3 above, failures and change requests lead to additional development, integration and testing activities. This must be planned, set up and monitored at the operational layer. This phase ends with the approval of the concept proposal, the system concept changes and the planning document in quality gate Q_A;

(b) **Requirements and impact analysis**: Similar to phases 4 and 5 above, the required changes need to be analysed and their impact on the existing functional and technical designs has to be considered and incorporated. This phase ends with the approval of the modified detailed design document in quality gate Q_B;

(c) **Bug fixing or product changes**: Similar to phase 5 above, the modifications of the detailed design document have to be translated into hardware, communications, and executable software. The modified software must be systematically retested to ensure its components and integration satisfy the product quality requirements. If necessary, hardware is re-assembled and re-tested to conform to the product quality model. This phase ends with the approval of the detailed test completion report in quality gate Q_C;

(d) **Integration & testing and regression testing**: Similar to phase 6 above, the various components of the system are integrated and systematically tested to conform to the product quality model. Here, functional as well as non-functional requirements have to be satisfied. Before installing and operating the system in a production environment, the system must undergo certification and accreditation activities, if necessary. This phase ends with the approval of the detailed integration and test completion report in quality gate Q_D;

(e) **Implementation**: Similar to phase 7 above, the system is installed and made operational in the production environment. This phase continues until the modified system landscape is operating in production in accordance with the defined requirements. This phase ends with the approval of the acceptance by Operations in quality gate Q_E.

9. **Disposal**: Disposal activities ensure the orderly termination of the system and preserve vital information about the system so that some or all of the information can be reactivated in the future if necessary—also known as "digital preservation". Particular emphasis is given to proper preservation of the data processed by the system, so that the data is effectively migrated to another system or archived in accordance with applicable records management regulations and policies, for potential future access. This phase ends with the approval of the long-term archive of the system—removed from the production environment— by Operations in quality gate Q_9.

Note that this model does not in any way presuppose a particular development model. It could be Agile, waterfall or any other suitable model. But we strongly believe that a lifecycle is always sequential and closed because it starts with the needs for a product and ends with its disposal. In between, we may have iterations, cycles or sprints. The corresponding processes within such a lifecycle model can be adapted and tailored from SPICE (ISO 2011), CMMI (Chrissis et al. 2011), ISO 9001 (2008), EFQM (2012) or even a combination of these.

For further discussion, it is also important to bear in mind that the impact of not having the right quality in place increases from left to right.

2.4 Third "P": Products

The third "P" stands for Products, which usually mean the goods and services offered by an enterprise (cf. Fig. 2.1). Generally speaking it is the "what" of reaching a particular goal. In our case the term product will be used as it is in manufacturing; products for us are the input and output artefacts of the whole lifecycle. Therefore, it could be software offered by software companies or developed by an enterprise itself and implemented afterwards; it could also be apps from an app-store or even a complete ICT systems landscape of a global enterprise. What it really means in given situations depends on the goals and perspectives of the observer. We will discuss our product view along two lines, the lifecycle (horizontal structure) and the vertical structure of enterprise ICT. In doing so, we will restrict ourselves to the most relevant products from a quality perspective. Of course, those products have to be validated or verified. This will be discussed later on.

Along the lifecycle (cf. Figure 2.5): Remember that phases 3–7 are mostly organised in a project setting with clear targets, scopes and schedules.

Therefore, project order, project charter and project plan are sample products generated by phase 2. Projects that are not organised using traditional methods, like PMI (2013), but those like Scrum (Pilcher 2008), will still produce the same products, even if the corresponding products are named differently. In an ICT project (phases 3–7) the requirements specification, the functional design, the technical design, the software, the test-ware and the implementation guide are the most important products. They also need right quality for future modifications and strongly influence the costs of operations and maintenance. As it concerns the development and maintenance phase of the whole ICT landscape, the products of phase 8 are similar to the products of a project (see above). The particular products affected depend on the type of task that has to be undertaken; bug fixing, implementation of change requests or implementation of new products. For example, bug fixing has mostly no project organisation, whereas the development and implementation of new products that result from change requests are organised in projects.

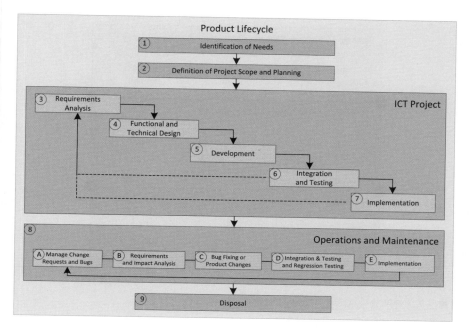

Fig. 2.5 Products along the lifecycle

***Along the vertical structure of enterprise ICT (cf. Figure** 2.6)*: Remember from above discussions that the vertical structure is a layered one consisting of the strategic, the tactical and the operational layer.

At the strategic layer we have products like the business processes mentioned above, which are clustered into business domains depending on the enterprise markets and target groups. Also included from a business perspective are the marketing and sales channels, through which a customer or user has access to the offerings and services of an enterprise. Different types of channels, so-called interaction levels, are well known (cf. von Lucke and Reinermann 2000): (1) *information type*, i.e. collecting data and information and providing it to the customers and users through applications like enterprise portals; (2) *communication type*, i.e. exchange of data and information between customers or users and the enterprise using additional services like blogs, forums, e-mail and video conferencing; (3) *transaction type*, i.e. order execution including the whole order processing and fulfilment using services like tracking and electronic payment. The object list at the strategic layer comes from portfolio management and especially from business process management. At the tactical layer we have products, like service architecture, consisting of service clusters, services and service components. The latter are often used not only in one but in many services or service clusters. The object list comes from application portfolio management and especially from enterprise architecture management. The business channels are handled by services

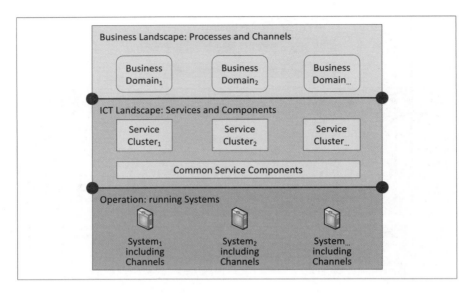

Fig. 2.6 Products along the vertical structure

and service components. The products at the operational layer are real-world objects, like an ICT system or application which serves the business channels by means of smartphones, tablets, laptops or PCs. Different types of channels need different types of implementations. The traditional type is implemented by an office or a branch. An example from retail banking might illustrate this vertical structure in more detail (cf. Fig. 2.7).

At the top level we have the customers, who choose a particular channel to get access to the services of a bank. Suppose the customer wants to take out a loan. In that case the corresponding "Retail lending" business process is performed through the selected channel. This process cluster is subdivided into three processes ("Loan origination", "Loan servicing" and "Loan closure"). Note that not all services are valid for every business channel. For example, "Receive application" is a service that is performed in the branch but not through internet.

Going down to the tactical layer we have the services and service components. Going down from this layer we reach the operational layer, where the corresponding systems run. This provides us with suitable object lists at the various layers of an enterprise. Hence, defining the right quality for every layer becomes possible and the corresponding methods, procedures and tools of quality governance, quality management and quality engineering can be applied. The question of how the required quality defined by the upper layer is to be validated and verified is then answered at the lower layer.

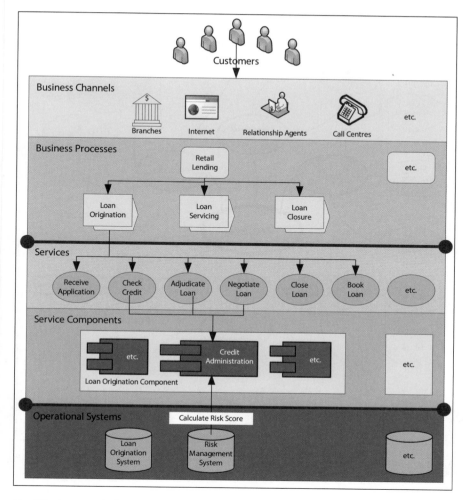

Fig. 2.7   An example from retail banking

2.5   Fourth "P": Projects and Portfolio

The fourth "P" stands for Projects and Portfolio. Projects are of set up, have certain goals and are limited to a planned budget. Generally speaking it is again the 'how' for reaching a particular goal. In our product lifecycle model (cf. Fig. 2.4) the phases from the beginning up to implementation normally make up at most 30 % of the effort to be spent on the product during the whole lifecycle. The rest of the effort, 70 %, is dedicated to the "operations and maintenance" phase. Usually the phases from requirements analysis up to implementation are organised in projects. Likewise, some tasks from the "operations and maintenance" phase will be

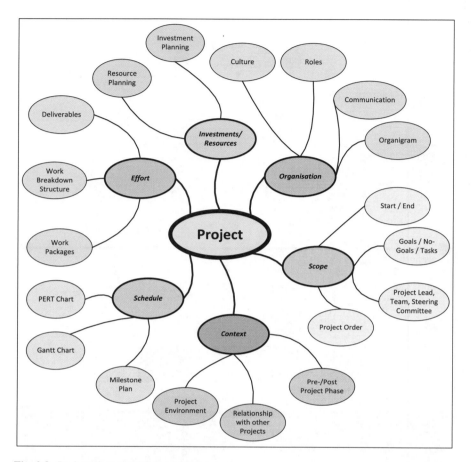

Fig. 2.8 Project elements for consideration

organised in projects. A proposal of lean maintenance for manufacturing (Harsey and Yusof 2011) can also help to improve this phase, but it is not our intention to discuss it here.

From project management methodologies like PMI (2013) we learn that many issues have to be considered before execution, although only a few of them are well known. Figure 2.8 provides examples of project elements that have to be taken into account when starting (cf. Sterrer and Winkler 2006 for a similar picture).

Due to the general complexity of projects, and failure rates far beyond 20 % for ICT projects specifically, new methodologies have appeared during the last decade. The Agile development paradigm, in particular, has heavily influenced planning and execution of projects (cf. for example Beck et al. 2001; Sutherland 2004; Sutherland 2005; and Pilcher 2008).

If we look for quality issues in such project management methodologies we find that most of them are rarely defined; no minimum quality requirements are predefined. Take for example the question of how much to invest in quality. Often it is less than budgeted, because the project lead decides to spend more money on development than on quality assurance, and it is less than needed, because quality is not regarded as a lifecycle issue (although everybody knows that costs dramatically increase in later phases of the lifecycle).

A far worse situation for many organisations is that project managers take a lot of heat when project management does not deliver "organisational nirvana". This is typical when executive leadership does not invest in the right selection of projects through the process of Project Portfolio Management.

Thus, the most common problem faced by project-oriented organisations is having too many projects relative to their capacity. Therefore, one of the first requirements is to determine what can be done; i.e. determine what should be done and what should not be done.

The Programme Management Survey 2002 (KPMG 2002) showed that 56 % of companies had a failed project within the preceding year at an average cost of £8 million. Other surveys indicate that up to 87 % of projects fail to deliver expected benefits. The problem is huge and yet companies are failing to address this issue effectively.

What we have found with our customers is that they have too many projects relative to their capacity and their approaches to the problem are:

- A piecemeal solution;
- Failure to appreciate and manage this at the portfolio level;
- Absence of corporate change culture;
- Absence of overall quality assurance.

The lack of coordination of strategic projects—also failing to recognise some initiatives as projects—leads to a dilution of resources, conflicting project objectives and ultimately not meeting their strategic objectives. We have found that companies need to understand that projects, programmes and portfolio need to be managed and supported in line with their development capability, as shown in Fig. 2.9, and this has to be supported across processes, people, tools and techniques.

Therefore, one of the first things is to determine what can be done; i.e. determine what should be done and what should not be done. Our experience tells us that organisations need Project Portfolio Management when there are:

- Too many projects in progress or uncertainty on how many there are;
- Uncertainty with regard to how projects support organisational strategy;
- Lack of priority balance; e.g., risk vs. timeframe;
- Questionable project value or project's value is disproportionate to investment;
- Resources working overtime while other resources are under-utilised;
- Lack of understanding of project interdependencies;
- Consistent failure to meet project cost, schedule, and technical milestones.

Research by Cooper, Edgett, and Kleinschmidt (1998) shows that the primary cause of business underachievement lies in failing to manage the collection of all projects as a portfolio. This problem is a direct result of the lack of an adequate

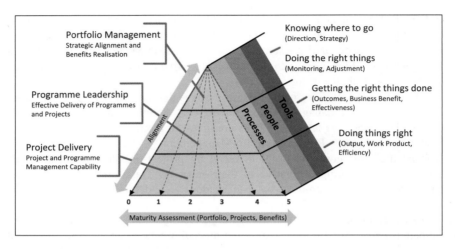

Fig. 2.9 Portfolio management

portfolio management process supported by enabling software. In our experience
most companies do not have processes or tools that provide the information needed
to make fact-based decisions about their portfolio of projects. As a result, senior
executives are in a constant dilemma and cannot answer the following questions
with confidence (or can confidently answer in the negative):

- Is my organisation working on the right projects and programmes?
- Are we working on the right number of projects and programmes?
- What resources do I need to complete the programmes as planned?
- Do we have effective processes in place to select and accomplish the
  programmes?
- When can I start a new programme?
- What is the impact of a new or modified programme schedule on lower priority
  programmes?
- What is the status of each project and programme?
- What is the history of schedule prediction vs. performance?

Another way to look at the problem is that most companies do not have fully
effective processes for making decisions about the portfolio of projects and most
companies do not have the supporting processes or tools that provide the information needed to make fact-based decisions about the portfolio of projects.

Benefits of Project Portfolio Management Concerning ICT Quality

There are many benefits of implementing Project Portfolio Management; however, there are three primary reasons why even the rank-and-file of project management should not only welcome PPM initiatives, but actively promote them at the grassroots level:

1. **PPM brings realism to an organisation's planning processes.** The Balanced Scorecard Collaborative estimates that upwards of 80 % of corporate strategies are never implemented. While the reasons for this are complex, at least part of the problem is that "strategic thinkers" dream up initiatives that the company has no hope of carrying out. Likewise, the hammering project management takes for "bad estimates" and project failure often begins in the executive suite with unrealistic targets, deadlines, and budgets. PPM aligns what an organisation wants to do with the resources—money, hours, people, time, and equipment—required for getting it done.
2. **PPM brings rationality in the allocation of resources, both human and financial.** After project inventory, the next important step in creating and executing a PPM process is to establish budgets (money and human resources), and define start and finish dates for these initiatives. Future projects or programmes are also forecasted and added to the organisation's potential portfolio of work. Also, at this stage, good PPM processes count heads. For some customers, the scarcest resource is not money but project managers. A critical factor in project selection is therefore: do we have a project manager who can manage it? This brings us to the third reason.
3. **PPM brings visibility of project work and project people.** The recent trend towards improved resource tracking and levelling functionality in project management software is a great boon to the project portfolio manager. In fact, without a system for knowing what each person in the pool of potential project staff is capable of, and when they will be available, you cannot really be said to manage a portfolio of projects.

So the fundamental task of ensuring the organisation launches the right quality initiatives requires first that the organisation aligns the projects with its business strategy. This is exactly what is achieved through the portfolio management process. The second step is creating checkpoints (quality gates) along the project lifecycle, where governance and exit criteria are in healthy balance. This results in an approach which we will call Portfolio Quality Management, as depicted in Fig. 2.10. For more details on portfolio management we refer to Rajegopal (2013).

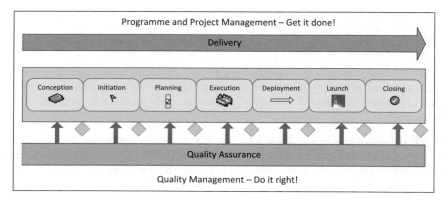

Fig. 2.10 PQM—Get it Done and Do it Right

References and Links

Barrett R (1998) Liberating the corporate soul: building a visionary organization. Butterworth-Heinemann, Woburn
Barrett R (2006) Building a values-driven organization: a whole system approach to cultural transformation. Elsevier, Oxford
Beck K et al (2001) The Agile Manifesto. http://www.agilemanifesto.org. Retrieved 7 Nov 2013
Chen K (2009) Product, project, process, and people: The four Ps of PLM analytics. http://www.technologyevaluation.com/research/articles/product-project-process-and-people-the-four-ps-of-plm-analytics-19934/. Retrieved 7 Nov 2013
Chrissis M, Konrad M, Shrum S (2011) CMMI for development: guidelines for process integration and product improvement, 3rd edn. Pearson Education, Boston, MA
Cooper R, Edgett S, Kleinschmidt E (1998) Portfolio management for new products. Perseus Books, Cambridge, MA
EFQM (2012) EFQM excellence model 2013. European Foundation for Quality Management (EFQM), Brussels
Hares J (1992) Information engineering for the advanced practitioner. Wiley, Chichester
Harsey F, Yusof S (2011) Continuous Improvement through an integrated maintenance model. In: Contemporary engineering sciences, vol 4(8). Hikari Ltd, Ruse Bulgaria, pp 353–362
Heinrich L, Lehner F (2005) Informationsmanagement: Planung, Überwachung und Steuerung der Informationsinfrastruktur. Oldenbourg Verlag, München
ISO (2011) Information technology—process assessment, ISO/IEC 15504. International Organization for Standardization (ISO), Geneva
ISO 9001 (2008) Qualitätsmanagementsysteme—Anforderungen, ISO 9001:2008. International Organization for Standardization (ISO), Geneva
KPMG (2002) Programme management survey. KPMG, London
Krcmar H (2005) Informationsmanagement. Springer, Berlin
Pilcher R (2008) Scrum—Agiles Projektmanagement erfolgreich einsetzen. dpunkt.verlag, Heidelberg
PMI (2013) The standard for program management, 3rd edn. Project Management Institute, Newtown Square, PA
Rajegopal S (2013) Portfolio management—how to innovate and invest in successful projects. Palgrave Macmillan, Basingstoke, Hampshire
Spring M (1992) People, processes, products and productivity—an address to EDGE International. http://www.sis.pitt.edu/~spring/papers/pppp.pdf. Retrieved 13 Nov 2013

Stafford P (2013) Nasdaq blames software flaw for trading outage. http://www.ft.com/intl/cms/s/0/138ccd6c-10c7-11e3-b5e4-00144feabdc0.html#axzz2l04nskPC. Retrieved 7 Nov 2013

Sterrer C, Winkler G (2006) Let your projects fly. Goldegg Verlag, Wien

Sutherland J (2004) Agile development: lessons learned from the First Scrum (The article was published by the Cutter Agile Project Management Advisory Service. Executive Update, Vol. 5, No. 20. Contact service@cutter.com for reprints)

Sutherland J (2005) Future of Scrum: parallel pipelining of sprints in complex projects. In: AGILE 2005 conference, Denver

US Department of Justice (2003) Information resources management—the Department of justice systems development life cycle guidance document. http://www.justice.gov/jmd/irm/lifecycle/table.htm. Retrieved 13 Nov 2013

von Lucke J, Reinermann H (2000) Speyerer Definition von Electronic Government. http://foev.dhv-speyer.de/ruvii/Sp-EGov.pdf. Retrieved 18 Nov 2013

http://femgineer.com/wp-content/uploads/2010/03/Shuttle_launch.jpg. Retrieved 21 Dec 2013

Chapter 3
What Is Right Software and Systems Quality?

Of course, the software industry has accepted that quality of ICT systems is important. A variety of tools have been made available to conduct computer-aided verification and validation of the respective artefacts. Most of them are dedicated to dynamic testing and static code quality control. The tools themselves cover an array of testing capabilities, and span the dynamics of various scenarios across projects and application development environments through production systems.

Usually projects or programmes are initiated to enhance, replace, maintain or improve software-based systems. Such projects and programmes have defined goals and frame conditions which are mostly directed to functionality, budget and time. But the question of where quality requirements come from must also be asked. Functionality itself is not a quality characteristic, but completeness of the specified functionality, for instance, is. We believe that a notion of right quality should be defined which serves the needs of quality in projects and programmes but which also conforms to the quality requirements in the lifecycle. We also believe that properties of software-based systems change over time and in response to changing stakeholder expectations.

Two sources have inspired us in defining a notion of right quality: the International Standard ISO/IEC 25010—as part of the SQuaRE series—and the Kano model. We will discuss our notion of "Right Software and Systems Quality" along the following questions:

1. What are the determining factors of quality?
2. Which quality characteristics and quality models are relevant?
3. Do quality requirements change over time and in response to stakeholder expectations?
4. What, then, is Right Software and Systems Quality?

M. Wieczorek et al., *Systems and Software Quality*,
DOI 10.1007/978-3-642-39971-8_3, © Springer-Verlag Berlin Heidelberg 2014

3.1   Determining Factors of Quality

Awareness for quality of software-based systems is not really perfected and it is widely accepted that we cannot get "absolute quality". Quality of a system and its components is relative and what we need is a methodology to reach a suitable level of quality which can be made transparent at all different layers of an enterprise and which is affordable under a given framework and environmental conditions.

Quality is by nature multi-dimensional and involves a sequence of compromises. Quality consists of many different properties, which are not always independent of each other. Some of these properties are easy to measure, like "the reaction time of a program on a request is within 10 seconds" whereas other properties like "the colour of a control on a screen must be red" are more ambiguous and are discerned by the individual. What one person sees as high quality may be considered by another individual as a low standard of quality.

Unlike budget and time, quality is a notion which is not easy to define. That makes it difficult to delineate quality and leads to workarounds such as "good quality is delivered when all test cases are executed and no serious errors occur at the end". Does this really give us an accurate indication of the quality of the system? Obviously it does not, because we do not know the quality of the test cases. We can follow this argumentation and try to find out the quality of the test cases and so on. But is this reasoning useful? What is mostly missing is that we do not have suitable transparency about the quality because of the complexity of the product and the complexity of the processes. This leads to two important questions:

1. Is the product (software-based system) the right one?
2. Assuming the product to be the right one, does it have the right quality?

The first question focuses on business characteristics, i.e. which business products and business processes have to be managed and supported by the software-based system, and is the software-based system the right one to do this efficiently. The second question focuses on the characteristics of a software-based system assuming that the system has the right business characteristics. The goals of all quality actions to be taken are then:

Make transparent whether there are risks when applying the product and give detailed indicators of those risks so that they can either be prevented as early as possible or at least be mitigated in their impacts.

Fundamental to all further discussions is an appropriate notion of software and systems quality. Out of practical needs, many different quality concepts and models have been defined over recent years (cf. for example Schmitz et al. 1982; Kan 1995; and Grady and Caswell 1987).

In this book we will take the International Standards of the SQuaRE series as a foundation. In ISO/IEC 25010 (2011), the quality of a (software-based) system is defined as

"... the degree to which the system satisfies the stated and implied needs of its various stakeholders, and thus provides value. These stated and implied needs are represented ... by quality models that categorize product quality into characteristics, which in some cases are further subdivided into sub-characteristics."

The International Standard provides a breakdown of quality into characteristics, sub-characteristics—and maybe more layers—and quality properties. All this defines a concrete quality model to which a certain software, system or product in a particular case has to adhere. Additionally, a distinction is made between "system/ software product quality models" and "quality-in-use models". The first type of models will be applied to software and systems when it is seen as a product; and the second type of models will be applied to software and systems when the view of different stakeholders is important. These two model types will be different and deliver extra information for the overall quality. In our view, the first one is more directed to the development and the second more to planning and use of software and systems.

In ISO/IEC 25012 (2008), data quality is defined according to two viewpoints— inherent data quality and system-dependent data quality.

"Inherent data quality refers to the degree to which quality characteristics of data have the intrinsic potential to satisfy stated and implied needs when data is used under specified conditions."

"System-dependent data quality refers to the degree to which data quality is reached and preserved within a computer system when data is used under specified conditions."

A good summary and discussion is also provided in Wagner (2013). Nevertheless, let us briefly discuss the two quality models here because they are fundamental for subsequent exercises in this book:

Quality-in-Use Model (QiUMod): The quality-in-use model consists of five characteristics where most characteristics have further sub-characteristics. The latter will not be discussed in detail (cf. ISO/IEC 25010 2011).

1. Effectiveness: accuracy and completeness with which users achieve specified goals; this is about getting the right things from the system in use supporting the corresponding business process or part of it; no further sub-characteristics are defined;
2. Efficiency: resources expended in relation to the accuracy and completeness with which users achieve goals; relevant resources may include time to complete a task, materials, or even financial costs of use; this is about getting the right things in the right way without wasting resources; no further sub-characteristics are defined;
3. Satisfaction: degree to which user needs are fulfilled when a product or system is used in a specified context of use; this is about conflicting areas like "getting what is needed" vs. "getting what is required" or "getting what is developed"; this characteristic is refined by usefulness, trust, pleasure and comfort at the user interface;

4. Freedom from risk: degree to which a product or system mitigates potential risks; these risks are subdivided into economic risk mitigation, health and safety risk mitigation and environmental risk mitigation (remember our discussions about the ICT and the embedded worlds in Chap. 1);
5. Context coverage: degree to which a product or system can be used with effectiveness, efficiency, freedom from risk, and satisfaction in specified contexts of use as well as contexts beyond those initially explicitly identified; this characteristic is subdivided into context completeness and flexibility (remember again our discussions about the ICT and the embedded worlds in Chap. 1).

In our view, "freedom from risk" is equivalent to "delivered high quality". If high quality is expressed by characteristics one, two, three and five above then freedom from risk is strongly dependent on those characteristics. Hence, it may be better in the future to derive this characteristic from the others and not to make it part of the definition itself.

Product Quality Model (ProdQMod): The product quality model consists of eight characteristics where each is further refined by sub-characteristics. Here, too, the sub-characteristics will not be discussed in detail (cf. ISO/IEC 25010 2011).

1. Functional suitability: degree to which a product or system provides functions that meet stated and implied needs when used under specified conditions; this characteristic is subdivided into functional completeness, functional correctness and functional appropriateness;
2. Performance efficiency: performance relative to the amount of resources used under stated conditions; resources may include other software products, the software and hardware configuration of the system and materials like print paper and storage media; human resources are not included here; this characteristic is further subdivided into time behaviour, resource utilisation and capacity;
3. Compatibility: degree to which a product or system or system component can exchange information with other products, systems or system components, and/or perform its required functions, while sharing the same hardware or software environment; this is subdivided into co-existence and interoperability;
4. Usability: degree to which a product or system can be used by specified users to achieve specified goals with effectiveness, efficiency, and satisfaction in a specified context of use; this is subdivided into appropriateness recognisability, learnability, operability, user error protection, user interface aesthetics and accessibility;
5. Reliability: degree to which a product, system, or system component performs specified functions under specified conditions for a specified period of time; limitations are due to faults in requirements, design and implementation, or due to contextual changes; wear does not occur in software but in systems where hardware is part of the system; this characteristic is further subdivided into maturity, availability, fault tolerance and recoverability;
6. Security: degree to which a product or system protects information and data so that people or other products or systems have the degree of data access appropriate to their types and levels of authorisation; this applies to both data storage

and data transmission; this is subdivided into confidentiality, integrity, non-repudiation, accountability and authenticity;

7. Maintainability: degree of effectiveness and efficiency with which a product or system can be modified by the intended maintainers; modifications include corrections, improvements, or adaptations of the software to changes in environment, in requirements, and in functional specifications; installation of updates and upgrades is included; this characteristic is further subdivided into modularity, reusability, analysability, modifiability and testability;

8. Portability: degree of effectiveness and efficiency with which a product, system, or system component can be transferred from one hardware, software or other operational or usage environment to another; this is subdivided into adaptability, installability and replaceability.

As a summary we have depicted all the characteristics together with their respective sub-characteristics in Fig. 3.1. It may be the case in specific contexts that additional, context-dependent standards and characteristics have to be satisfied. In that case, the above mechanism of quality models can be extended.

Data Quality Model (DataQMod): Setting aside the two viewpoints mentioned above, a data quality model consists of the following characteristics [for more details refer to ISO/IEC 25012 (2008)].

1. Accuracy: Degree to which data has attributes that correctly represent the true value of the intended attributes of a concept or event in a specific context of use;
2. Accessibility: Degree to which data can be accessed in a specific context of use, particularly by people who need supporting technology or a special configuration because of some disability;
3. Availability: Degree to which data has attributes that enable it to be retrieved by authorised users and/or applications in a specific context of use;
4. Completeness: Degree to which subject data associated with an entity has values for all expected attributes and related entity instances in a specific context of use;
5. Consistency: Degree to which data has attributes that are free from contradiction and are coherent with other data in a specific context of use;
6. Credibility: Degree to which data has attributes that are regarded as true and believable by users in a specific context of use;
7. Currentness: Degree to which data has attributes that are of the right age in a specific context of use;
8. Compliance: Degree to which data has attributes that adhere to applicable standards, conventions or regulations and similar rules relating to data quality in a specific context of use;
9. Confidentiality: Degree to which data has attributes that ensure that it is only accessible and interpretable by authorised users in a specific context of use;
10. Efficiency: Degree to which data has attributes that can be processed and provide the expected levels of performance by using the appropriate amounts and types of resources in a specific context of use;

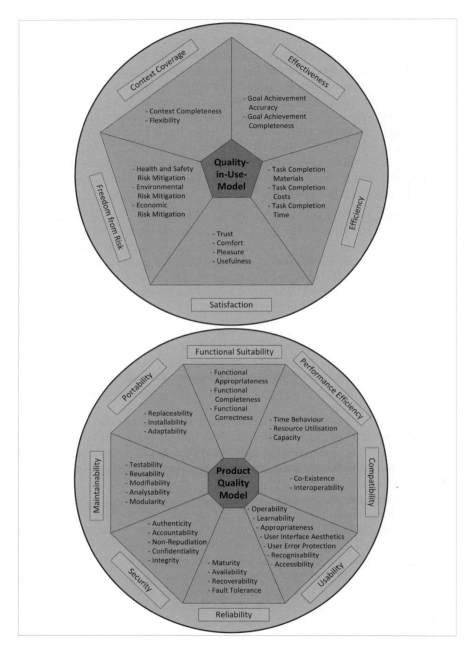

Fig. 3.1 Quality-in-use model and product quality model

11. Portability: Degree to which data has attributes that enable it to be installed, replaced or moved from one system to another while preserving the existing quality in a specific context of use;
12. Precision: Degree to which data has attributes that are exact or that provide discrimination in a specific context of use;
13. Recoverability: Degree to which data has attributes that enable it to maintain and preserve a specified level of operations and quality, even in the event of failure, in a specific context of use;
14. Traceability: Degree to which data has attributes that provide an audit trail of access to the data and of any changes made to the data in a specific context of use;
15. Understandability: Degree to which data has attributes that enable it to be read and interpreted by users, and are expressed in appropriate languages, symbols and units in a specific context of use.

As a summary we have depicted all the characteristics together with their respective sub-characteristics in Fig. 3.2. It may be the case in specific contexts that additional, context-dependent standards and characteristics have to be satisfied.

Process Quality Model (ProcQMod): A process quality model usually consists of the relevant processes including their definitions, capability levels and process attributes (for more details refer to the SPICE standard ISO/IEC 15504-1 2004; ISO/IEC 15504-4 2004; ISO/IEC 15504-5 2012; and ISO/IEC 15504-7 2008 or Chrissis et al. 2011). For example, SPICE defines processes within five categories, customer/supplier, engineering, supporting, management and organisation. Process attributes such as process performance, performance management, work product management, process definition, process deployment, process measurement, process control, process innovation and process optimisation are defined for these processes. With such definitions it is then possible to assess each attribute on a four-point (N-P-L-F) rating scale:

- Not achieved (0–15 %);
- Partially achieved (>15–50 %);
- Largely achieved (>50–85 %);
- Fully achieved (>85–100 %).

The capability level of all or a selected number of processes can then be determined for an enterprise with the following scale of capability levels:

- Incomplete process—capability level 0;
- Performed process—capability level 1;
- Managed process—capability level 2;
- Established process—capability level 3;
- Predictable process—capability level 4;
- Optimising process—capability level 5.

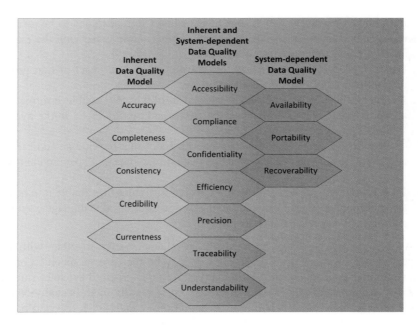

Fig. 3.2 Inherent data quality model and system-dependent data quality model

3.2   Relevance of Quality Characteristics

Are all the quality characteristics of the above models equally important or does their relevance depend on contextual properties? For example, as part of the "People" category (cf. Chap. 2) we have differentiated stakeholder groups where each has its own view and expectations on quality. Moreover, "user experience and role" seems to be important when asking for ranking quality characteristics. Another example belongs to the "Product" category (cf. Chap. 2). Looking into the lifecycle processes we have identified many different products/artefacts that contribute to the structure and behaviour of ICT systems. If the application is under development the ranking might be different from the ranking when the same application has been running for 10 years. So the "age of an application" is a driving factor, too. Take for example the Microsoft Office application. If you are running an old version, say MS Office 2000, the fundamental platform may no longer be supported and you may have issues with performance and reliability with current desktop versions. A similar argumentation is true for applications like SAP and PLM.

Let us start our investigation into rankings of quality characteristics with the quality-in-use model. Remember that this model provides the "user" perspective on quality. It is determined by the whole system consisting of hardware, software and operating environment—including user and operator manuals and first and second level support—as well as the user himself, his tasks and his social environment.

Table 3.1   A sample ranking of quality-in-use characteristics

	Effectiveness	Efficiency	Satisfaction	Freedom from Risk	Context Coverage	Total Rate
Effectiveness		3	2	3	3	11
Efficiency	1		3	3	3	10
Satisfaction	2	1		3	3	9
Freedom from Risk	1	1	1		3	6
Context Coverage	1	1	1	1		4

The model does not focus on the system itself, but requires and expects certain contextual properties coming from the usage of the system (Table 3.1). For convenience of our evaluation, we will make use of a three-value rating scheme with the following meaning:

- 3—more critical if not present during production;
- 2—equally critical during production;
- 1—less critical if not present during production.

The contextual properties are given by the "user" stakeholder. The assignment of values comes from over 7,000 projects and can be interpreted as "the majority of projects have chosen the corresponding value". For example, in most of the projects effectiveness ("accuracy and completeness with which users achieve specified goals") and satisfaction ("degree to which user needs are fulfilled when a product or system is used in a specified context of use") are equally important although satisfaction ranks third in the overall table. This is because satisfaction is ranked as less critical in relation to efficiency ("resources expended in relation to the accuracy and completeness with which users achieve goals"). Such a ranking is important for scalable, risk-based quality assurance approaches to optimise the investment.

Another view is provided by the product quality model, which is intended to look at product properties of the corresponding system. This is more than just looking at it from a user's perspective. For example, internal quality such as code quality is incorporated here but not in the quality-in-use model. For convenience of our evaluation, we will make use of a similar rating scheme as above:

- 3—more critical if the product/system does not satisfy the particular quality requirement;
- 2—equally critical if the product/system does not satisfy the particular quality requirement;
- 1—less critical if the product/system does not satisfy the particular quality requirement.

First, let us look at legacy applications. A sample ranking is depicted in Table 3.2.

If a certain product quality characteristic is more critical than another one then the risk level is, in general, much higher. For example, characteristics like functional suitability and usability will be more critical than maintainability or performance efficiency. Host applications like retail lending (cf. Chap. 2) are more dependent on functional suitability, performance efficiency and security.

Table 3.2 A sample ranking of product quality characteristics for legacy applications

	Functional Suitability	Reliability	Performance Efficiency	Usability	Security	Compatibility	Maintainability	Portability	Total Rate
Functional Suitability		2	3	3	2	3	3	3	19
Reliability	2		3	3	2	3	3	3	19
Performance Efficiency	1	1		3	3	3	3	3	17
Usability	1	1	1		3	3	3	3	15
Security	2	2	1	1		3	3	3	15
Compatibility	1	1	1	1	1		2	2	9
Maintainability	1	1	1	1	1	2		2	9
Portability	1	1	1	1	1	2	2		9

If we now make a distinction between several types of applications, some interesting effects occur. We asked people who use applications with high customer interaction, e.g. consumer software, for a ranking of product quality characteristics and we got the results shown in Table 3.3.

In this case, quality characteristics are more directed to usability, performance efficiency and reliability. Functional suitability is less important and also technical properties like maintainability are ranked lower.

Similarly, we asked people from the SAP field to rank the product quality characteristics, again using the pairwise comparison tool. Although not representative, the results depicted in Table 3.4 give an idea of the importance of the various quality characteristics.

In this SAP case, quality characteristics are more directed to functional suitability, security, usability and maintainability. Less important are technical properties like compatibility and portability.

Similarly, we asked people from the PLM field to rank the product quality characteristics using the pairwise comparison tool. Again, though not representative, the results depicted in Table 3.5 give an idea of the importance of the various quality characteristics. A slightly different procedure has been followed here. We will review this from a pure user perspective and from a product company perspective. Each cell therefore contains two values, the left one represents the product company perspective and the right one represents the user perspective.

As expected, the results are different. In the case of the user perspective the most important characteristic is security, whereas in the product company perspective it is functional suitability and reliability. The results for compatibility, maintainability and portability were somewhat surprising to us. From a product company viewpoint most of the costs go to maintenance. If different platforms come into existence it is also a cost factor if different codes have to be maintained. We were also surprised to see usability as being less important for a user than for a product company.

In concluding this section about rankings of quality characteristics—legacy systems, multi-channel applications, ERP systems and PLM solutions—we arrive

Table 3.3 A sample ranking of product quality characteristics for multi-channel applications

	Functional Suitability	Reliability	Performance Efficiency	Usability	Security	Compatibility	Maintainability	Portability	Total Rate
Functional Suitability		2	3	2	1	3	2	3	16
Reliability	2		3	3	1	3	2	2	16
Performance Efficiency	1	1		2	1	3	3	3	14
Usability	2	1	2		1	3	3	3	15
Security	3	3	3	3		3	3	3	21
Compatibility	1	1	1	1	1		2	2	9
Maintainability	2	2	1	1	1	2		2	11
Portability	1	2	1	1	1	2	2		10

Table 3.4 A sample ranking of product quality characteristics for ERP applications

	Functional Suitability	Reliability	Performance Efficiency	Usability	Security	Compatibility	Maintainability	Portability	Total Rate
Functional Suitability		2	3	3	1	2	3	3	17
Reliability	2		3	3	1	2	3	3	17
Performance Efficiency	1	1		3	1	1	1	3	11
Usability	1	1	1		1	1	1	2	8
Security	3	3	3	3		3	3	3	21
Compatibility	2	3	3	3	1		2	3	17
Maintainability	2	3	3	3	1	2		3	17
Portability	1	1	1	2	1	1	1		8

Table 3.5 A sample ranking of product quality characteristics for PLM applications

	Functional Suitability	Reliability	Performance Efficiency	Usability	Security	Compatibility	Maintainability	Portability	Total Rate
Functional Suitability		2 / 2	2 / 2	2 / 2	1 / 1	2 / 3	3 / 3	3 / 3	18 / 16
Reliability	2 / 2		3 / 2	3 / 2	2 / 2	3 / 3	2 / 3	3 / 3	18 / 17
Performance Efficiency	1 / 2	1 / 2		1 / 2	1 / 2	2 / 3	2 / 3	3 / 3	11 / 17
Usability	1 / 2	1 / 2	3 / 2		1 / 2	1 / 3	2 / 3	2 / 3	11 / 17
Security	2 / 3	2 / 2	3 / 2	3 / 2		2 / 3	2 / 3	3 / 3	17 / 18
Compatibility	2 / 1	1 / 1	2 / 1	3 / 1	2 / 1		3 / 2	3 / 2	16 / 9
Maintainability	1 / 1	2 / 1	2 / 1	2 / 1	2 / 1	1 / 2		3 / 2	13 / 9
Portability	1 / 1	1 / 1	1 / 1	2 / 1	1 / 1	1 / 2	1 / 2		8 / 9

Table 3.6 Sample comparison of product quality characteristics for different types of applications

Rank	Legacy	Multi-Channel	ERP	PLM (user perspective)	PLM (product perspective)
1	Functional Suitability	Security	Security	Security	Functional Suitability
2	Reliability	Functional Suitability	Functional Suitability	Reliability	Reliability
3	Performance Efficiency	Reliability	Reliability	Performance Efficiency	Security
4	Usability	Usability	Compatibility	Usability	Compatibility
5	Security	Performance Efficiency	Maintainability	Functional Suitability	Maintainability
6	Compatibility	Maintainability	Performance Efficiency	Compatibility	Performance Efficiency
7	Maintainability	Portability	Usability	Maintainability	Usability
8	Portability	Compatibility	Portability	Portability	Portability

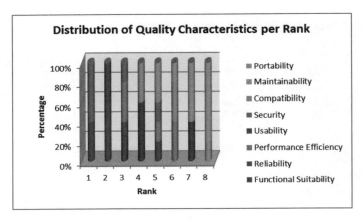

Fig. 3.3 Distribution of product quality characteristics

at the following interesting result (cf. Table 3.6). Note that all the rankings are based on our experiences made from projects over recent years.

Functional suitability is ranked top for legacy systems, for SAP industry solutions and also for PLM solutions, whereas this characteristic is less important for customer-focused applications. Here, usability is ranked top. Internal quality, i.e. maintainability, shows a heterogeneous picture. It is less important for legacy systems and for customer-focused applications, whereas it has a higher ranking for SAP and PLM solutions. Compatibility and portability do not seem to play a significant role. All these rankings might be different in different companies or in the future when considering other types of applications (i.e. mobile applications).

From Fig. 3.3 we learn that functional suitability and security are the most important characteristics. They are focused on projects where quality assurance is conducted. We also learn that portability is the least important characteristic.

3.3 Quality Models in the Lifecycle

A house is not built in 1 day, but there must be a framework and conditions to which everyone adheres during construction and maintenance. The governance framework and conditions are provided by the quality models in the lifecycle of every product or system and the lifecycle processes. There are a number of process quality models for the lifecycle processes. We suggest taking for example the SPICE model mentioned above.

As discussed above and also defined in Wagner (2013), quality models serve to describe, plan, predict and assess quality of software-based systems. Whereas the International Standards ISO/IEC 25010 (2011) and ISO/IEC 25012 (2008) provide quality models from a user, product and data perspective, we believe that during the lifecycle certain quality models must be distinguishable. These depend on the various artefact types and the lifecycle phase. This differentiation will help to implement product quality models appropriately and supports implementing industrialisation to setup a suitable service portfolio for a Quality Services Factory (cf. Chaps. 5 and 6). Of course, all such models are more or less refinements, extractions or enhancements of the product quality model as discussed above. Doing so gives us the opportunity for refinement and aggregation during vertical and horizontal integration into enterprise ICT quality (cf. Chap. 4).

During the lifecycle of an ICT system many different artefacts emerge. Table 3.7 provides an overview of how these models can be applied in the product lifecycle. We have included some significant artefact types, but the list is not comprehensive.

For example, assessing the architecture of a system is different from assessing the source code or the data used in databases. Some properties of artefacts can be assessed using structural (static) methods, e.g. source code quality, whereas properties of other artefacts can only be assessed if the behaviour of the corresponding system is considered, e.g. the complete system and its interaction within the ICT systems landscape and maybe with other systems outside the enterprise itself.

Documentation quality model (DocQMod): During the lifecycle different documentation types emerge. Documentation is either written as part of development and implementation to get the right product or as part of the product itself. Documentation may differ from one development model to another—e.g. VM-XT and agile—or from one enterprise to another but this is beyond our purposes in this book. The "documentation quality model" serves three purposes:

1. Be clear about the demands a particular documentation has to fulfil;
2. Provide the reference for verification of documentation;
3. Guide in selecting suitable methods for verification.

A practically proven approach for a DocQMod which we applied e.g. during the acceptance phase of a complex and long-lasting project contains the following quality characteristics:

- Completeness;
- Correctness;

Table 3.7 Artefacts and the corresponding quality models in the lifecycle

	Lifecycle Phase	Artefact Type	Quality Model
P1	Identification of Needs	Needs documentation	DocQMod
P2	Definition of Project Scope and Planning	Project documentation	DocQMod
P3	Requirements Analysis	Business process portfolio	BPQMod
		Requirements specification	ReqQMod
P4	Functional and Technical Design	Architecture model	ArchQMod
		Data model	DataQMod
P5	Development	Software documentation	DocQMod
		Source code	CodeQMod
		Databases	DataQMod
		System	SysQMod
P6	Integration and Testing	Test documentation	DocQMod
		Source code	CodeQMod
		Databases	DataQMod
		Environments including hardware	EnvQMod
		System cluster	SysQMod
P7	Implementation	Rollout documentation	DocQMod
		Source code	CodeQMod
		Databases	DataQMod
		System landscape	SysQMod
P8	Operations & Maintenance	Product documentation	DocQMod
		Productive system (ICT landscape)	QiUMod
		Other documentation (e.g. project)	DocQMod
		Test documentation	DocQMod
		Source code	CodeQMod
		Databases	DataQMod
		System	SysQMod
P9	Disposal	Archive (including documentation, business processes, source code, databases, environments)	DigPresQMod

- Unambiguity;
- Relevance;
- Clear structure;
- Compliance with rules and standards;
- Application of pre-defined methods and tools;
- Manageability (by release management).

Business process quality model (BPQMod): Software-based systems are built to enable and optimise the performance of business processes. The business processes define a way through which an enterprise will be successful. Therefore, single business processes and the whole business process portfolio must adhere to quality characteristics. There are a few characteristics which are specific for a business process portfolio, e.g. dependability matrix. Nevertheless, we will focus here on single business processes. The "business process quality model" serves three purposes:

1. Be clear about the demands a particular business process has to fulfil;
2. Provide the reference for verification of business processes;
3. Guide in selecting suitable methods for verification.

A practically proven approach for a BPQMod which we applied in many kinds of projects contains the following quality characteristics:

- Reliability;
- Completeness;
- Correctness;
- Understandability;
- Consistency;
- Validity;
- Currentness;
- Traceability;
- Prioritisation;
- Manageability (by release management).

Requirements quality model (ReqQMod): Requirements are one of the most important artefacts in the software and systems lifecycle. Moreover, requirements are most often the cause of errors and faults in productive system environments. If this is the case it costs a lot of effort to solve the problems in later phases of the lifecycle. We can distinguish requirements and requirements specifications in agreement with Rupp and die SOPHISTen (2007) but also in reference to Chen et al. (2013). There are a few characteristics that are specific for requirements specifications, e.g. sorting capability or common accessibility. Nevertheless, we restrict ourselves here to single requirements. The "requirements quality model" serves three purposes:

1. Be clear about the demands a particular requirement has to fulfil;
2. Provide the reference for verification of requirements;
3. Guide in selecting suitable methods for verification.

A practically proven approach for a ReqQMod which we applied in many kinds of projects contains the following quality characteristics:

- Completeness;
- Correctness;
- Non-repudiation;
- Consistency;
- Verifiability;
- Unambiguity;
- Understandability;
- Validity;
- Currentness;
- Feasibility;
- Necessity;
- Traceability;

- Prioritisation;
- Manageability (by release management).

Architecture quality model (ArchQMod): The architecture of a software-based system is a crucial link between business goals and the business process portfolio on the one hand and the running system on the other hand. Unfortunately, architecturally significant demands are often not specified or not communicated effectively (cf. Chen et al. 2013; Clerc 2009). Moreover, Clements et al. stated "There is a fundamental mismatch between the information that requirements specifications contain and the information that architects need." (cf. Clements and Bass 2010). The "architecture quality model" serves three purposes:

1. Be clear about the demands a particular architecture has to fulfil;
2. Provide the reference for verification of architectures;
3. Guide in selecting suitable methods for verification.

A practically proven approach for an ArchQMod which we applied in many kinds of assessments using ATAM (Kazman et al. 2000) contains the following quality characteristics:

- Availability;
- Usability;
- Modifiability;
- Compliance to standard architecture;
- Compliance to notation rules;
- Conformity with requirements/functional design;
- Performance (static view);
- Security (static view);
- Manageability (by release management).

Code quality model (CodeQMod): As we know from various publications, e.g. Simon et al. (2006), more than 60 % of the total cost of ownership for a software-based system is associated with maintenance effort, with about 50 % of this effort spent on understanding the code. A statement of the management summary from a project in 2013 gives a clear view on missing code quality, "there is a high risk that the technical debt will have a negative impact in the mid or long-term on development speed, failure rate and increased test effort". Code quality has become more prominent in the last couple of years. The "code quality model" serves three purposes:

1. Be clear about the demands which a particular code has to fulfil;
2. Provide the reference for verification of code;
3. Guide in selecting suitable methods for verification.

A practically proven approach for a CodeQMod which we applied in many kinds of projects contains the following quality characteristics:

- Time-behaviour
- Resource utilisation

- Maturity
- Fault tolerance
- Recoverability
- Analysability
- Modifiability
- Testability
- Modularity
- Adaptability
- Manageable through releases.

Data quality model (DataQMod): In our experience data quality is often neglected, which then leads to significant impacts in migration projects and production. But data is as important as functionality. As is well-known, applications cannot deliver any result if code (function) and data are not properly aligned. In the meantime data quality has also become part of ISO/IEC 25012 (2008) as mentioned above. The "data quality model" serves three purposes:

1. Be clear about the demands a particular database has to fulfil;
2. Provide the reference for verification of databases;
3. Guide in selecting suitable methods for verification.

A practically proven approach for a DataQMod which we applied in many kinds of projects contains the following quality characteristics:

- Accuracy;
- Availability;
- Completeness;
- Consistency;
- Credibility;
- Currentness;
- Accessibility;
- Compliance;
- Confidentiality;
- Efficiency;
- Portability;
- Precision;
- Recoverability;
- Traceability;
- Understandability;
- Manageability (by release management).

System quality model (SysQMod): In different phases of our lifecycle model we have different aggregations of software and system components. In Table 3.7 we have made a distinction between the "system", "system cluster" and "system landscape" artefact types. The system quality model is directed to the right behaviour of the respective artefact. The "system quality model" serves three purposes:

1. Be clear about the demands a particular system or component has to fulfil;
2. Provide the reference for verification of systems or components;
3. Guide in selecting suitable methods for verification.

A practically proven approach for a SysQMod which we applied in many kinds of projects contains the following quality characteristics:

• Functional completeness;
• Functional correctness;
• Functional appropriateness;
• Usefulness;
• Trust;
• Pleasure;
• Comfort;
• Testability;
• Manageability (by release management).

Environments quality model (EnvQMod): Environments here include e.g. hardware, server, networks, operating systems, database management systems and possibly other software components. Environments are often discussed and defined too late in projects; existing environments are often not suitable for the purposes required. The "environment quality model" serves three purposes:

1. Be clear about the demands a particular environment has to fulfil;
2. Provide the reference for verification of environments;
3. Guide in selecting suitable methods for verification.

A practically proven approach for an EnvQMod contains the following quality characteristics:

• Time behaviour;
• Resource utilisation;
• Capacity;
• Availability;
• Fault tolerance;
• Recoverability;
• Green IT;
• Manageability (by release management).

Digital preservation quality model (DigPresQMod): Requirements and detailed actions to be taken for digital preservation is the main part of the disposal phase of the lifecycle model (cf. Chap. 2). If the disposal does not plan for any preservation of digital objects then no quality model is required. But if there is a need for long-term preservation, the quality model depends on the kind of objects to be preserved. The Digital Preservation Europe group defines digital preservation as "a set of activities required to make sure digital objects can be located, rendered, used and understood in the future. This can include managing the object names and locations, updating the storage media, documenting the content and tracking hardware and software changes to make sure objects can still be opened and understood."

(cf. DPE 2013). They differentiate three kinds: preservation of bit streams, preservation of bit streams together with their meaning and preservation of understandable content in such a way that the provenance and source of the digital object also remains clear. The "digital preservation quality model" serves three purposes:

1. Be clear about the demands a particular digital preservation approach has to fulfil;
2. Provide the reference for verification of digital preservation approaches;
3. Guide in selecting suitable methods for verification.

From our viewpoint a practically relevant approach for a DigPresQMod should contain the following quality characteristics and therefore excludes certain approaches for digital preservation:

- Understandability;
- Readability;
- Usefulness;
- Authenticity;
- Accurateness;
- Completeness;
- Manageability (by release management).

3.4 Changing Quality Due to Time and Stakeholder Expectations

Does software and systems quality remain the same over time or does it change every time a project is set up that affects particular systems? Unlike the aging of certain wines, the internal quality of systems and software decreases over time if no actions are taken (cf. Lehman and Belady 1985). Therefore, we can say that a system's quality is in some sense also aging. Quality characteristics that are important at a certain point in time, e.g. when the first release goes live, will become less important in other phases of the lifecycle. For example, functional correctness is the most important property of a new system as indicated above. If such a system is modified over a five-year period due to bug-fixes and change requests then maintainability becomes more important because the cost factors put pressure on the ICT department.

In his famous paper (Kano et al. 1984), Kano describes a model for the relation between implementation degree and customer (user) satisfaction. This model is initially not defined with special attention to the software industry but we believe that it is attractive enough to provide some ideas. It has already been discussed in Agile approaches, but in our view the Kano model is independent of a particular project management or development approach. Essential to the Kano model are two dimensions: customer satisfaction and degree of implementation. Kano distinguishes three classes of features which are implementable and have impact on the

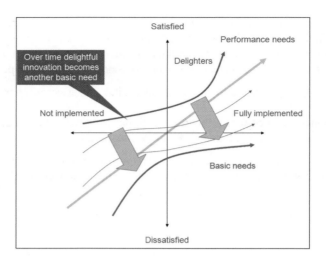

Fig. 3.4 Kano model including changes over time

satisfaction of the customers. This is also illustrated by Kano in Fig. 3.4 (retrieved from Kano 2013).

1. Basic attributes: these are basically the features a product must have in order to meet customer needs. If these attributes are missing, the product is simply incomplete and runs the risk of not being accepted. The product is being developed for some type of user base, and therefore this must be a crucial part of product innovation. If these attributes are not available, the product will soon leave the market due to dissatisfaction. The attribute is either there or not.
2. Performance attributes: a performance attribute is defined as a skill, knowledge, ability, or behavioural characteristic that is associated with job performance. Performance attributes are metrics on which a company bases its business aspirations. They have an explicit purpose. Companies prioritise their investments, decisions, and efforts and explain their strategies using performance attributes. Performance attributes are those for which more is better, and a better performance attribute will improve customer satisfaction. Conversely, a weak performance attribute reduces customer satisfaction. When customers discuss their needs, these needs fall into the performance attributes category. The attributes then form the weighted needs against the product concepts being evaluated. The price a customer is willing to pay for a product is closely tied to performance attributes. So the higher the performance attribute, the more the customers are willing to pay for the product.
3. Excitement attributes: these attributes are mostly unforeseen by the customer but may yield paramount satisfaction. The beauty behind an excitement attribute is to spur a potential customer's imagination; these attributes are used to help the customer discover needs they have never thought about before. The key behind the Kano model is for the engineer to discover these "unknown needs". The more the customer thinks about these amazing new ideas, the more they

want it. Of all the attributes introduced in the Kano model, the excitement ones are the most powerful and have the potential to lead to the highest gross profit margins. Innovation is undisputedly the catalyst in delivering these attributes to customers; we need to be able to distinguish what an excitement attribute is today, because tomorrow it becomes a known feature and the day after it is used throughout the whole world.

What changes over time and might have impact on software-based systems and their quality? For example, a customer's behaviour changes over time in that they will make use of new technology—think of various devices like smartphones and tablets. Will the existing applications have the right functionality and characteristics to deal with these new devices? Here, functionality should remain the same but required quality characteristics may shift to usability and performance. Therefore, if requirements change over time and systems are then modified to satisfy the new requirements, it is also important to know whether the quality requirements have changed and whether the quality models and the verification and validation assets also have to be adjusted. Strategically we would expect the characteristics to be more stable, and tactically it depends on the requested changes.

Of course, Kano applies his model to daily life products and their properties. How does it help us in our holistic quality approach? If stakeholders (customers/ users) change their expectations and priorities over time it will not be necessary to invest in those features—and their quality assurance—that are not as attractive as others. Therefore, we need to determine the risky and costly features to optimise the quality approach. To this end, questionnaires can be used to find out the "voice of the customer/user" (Hauser and Clausing 1988) and to document these features in the requirements specifications. Then the right link is given by the corresponding requirements quality model as discussed above. As argued in Sauerwein et al. (1996) for different products the usefulness of applying the Kano model in our approach becomes obvious. It is an important foundation for appropriate requirements specification and it gives rise to scalability and flexibility:

- Wide range of possibilities for differentiation: discovering and fulfilling exciting attributes creates a product which does not merely satisfy basic or performance attributes and is perceived as average and therefore interchangeable;
- Product development and quality engineering can be prioritised: as discussed above, it is not very useful to invest in improving a product which is already at a satisfactory level; instead it is better to improve characteristics as they have a greater influence on perceived product quality and consequently on the customer's level of satisfaction;
- Product requirements are better understood: the product criteria that have the greatest influence on customer satisfaction can be identified; classifying product requirements into must-be, one-dimensional and attractive dimensions can be used as a focal point;
- Tradeoff situations can better be resolved: if two requirements cannot be met simultaneously in the product development stage due to technical conditions, temporal dependencies or financial reasons, the criterion that has the greatest influence on customer satisfaction can be identified;

Table 3.8 Influence of product quality characteristics for a particular stakeholder

Product Quality Model	Quality-in-Use Model		
Characteristic	Primary User	Secondary User	Indirect User
Functional Suitability	strong	no	no
Reliability	middle	no	strong
Performance Efficiency	middle	middle	strong
Usability	middle	no	no
Security	middle	middle	strong
Compatibility	no	strong	no
Maintainability	no	strong	no
Portability	no	strong	no

- Customer-tailored solutions: special problems can be elaborated which guarantee an optimal level of satisfaction in the different customer segments.

We already discussed the influence of application types on quality characteristics. Another influence is given by the various stakeholders of an enterprise. We will briefly discuss this here according to the general product quality model (cf. ISO/IEC 25010 2011). It is also applicable to the artefact-dependent quality models as mentioned above. Product quality characteristics have a certain influence on quality-in-use depending on various stakeholders. There, a differentiation is made between "primary users", i.e. those who directly interact with the system in order to achieve primary goals, "secondary users", i.e. those who provide support to all the users of a system, and last but not least "indirect users", i.e. those who do not interact with the system but receive results from system interactions. Remember from Chap. 2 that the interaction type can differ between information, communication and transaction. This type obviously has an influence on the relevance of a characteristic on the quality-in-use perceived by a particular stakeholder. For operationalisation purposes, this differentiation can help to scale effort and cost for quality issues in a suitable way. An approximation from our experience is given in Table 3.8, which assumes influence categories "strong", "middle" and "no".

What now remains to be done is to find out the changes of the corresponding quality models. This gives rise to the maintenance of quality models (cf. Wagner 2013). Quality models are very similar to other artefacts of the lifecycle. They (should) reflect the voice of the corresponding stakeholder as long as the artefact exists in the product lifecycle. A quality model is valid or invalid at a certain point in time and in case of validity the corresponding artefact has to adhere to the quality requirements contained in such a model (cf. Fig. 3.5).

Thus, quality models underlie a continuous need of having the right models in place. Selecting the appropriate artefacts and defining the corresponding quality models including objects, characteristics, indicators and measures is often a challenge. We suggest using the Y-model approach of quality management and quality governance (cf. Simon and Simon 2010). A detailed description is provided in Chap. 5.

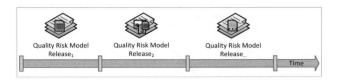

Fig. 3.5 Quality models evolving in time

3.5 Right Software and Systems Quality

As discussed above, quality is not an absolute notion but a relative one and it must be affordable. Will it be possible to have a notion of quality that allows for statements like "the ICT product has 80 % quality"? And if so, "which investment has to be taken so that 80 % product quality fits in the budget"? Let us look at the diagrams in Fig. 3.6. The V&V rules of the diagrams could be rules for verifying architecture or code as well as verifying the business suitability by dynamic testing.

For simplicity we presuppose the V&V rules to be a test case portfolio for dynamic testing of functional suitability of an application. If we execute more and more test cases we can be sure that the effort will increase infinitely. If we execute more and more test cases we would like to expect better quality but this is a fallacy as long as we do not know the coverage of the test cases. But it is indeed the case that if quality improves then more and more effort has to be spent. But what is the effect of such an investment? Is there an optimum where it does not make any sense to further increase effort, budgets or timeframe?

In Bourne (2012) Lynda Bourne discusses the total cost of quality from a PMO perspective. Two cost sources are mentioned here; cost of implementing quality and cost of rectifying defects. If both curves are plotted in one diagram as in Fig. 3.7, we can ascertain one point that is the optimum of the total cost for quality.

A similar view comes from Armand Feigenbaum. He differentiates in Feigenbaum (1991) between "cost of poor quality" and "cost of good quality". Our thinking is along similar lines: if quality is good then risk will be low and if quality is poor then risk will be high. With the notion of risk we can calculate quality in terms of risk, i.e. damage index multiplied by the probability that the damage will occur. Balancing cost of quality and cost of risk (damage) leads us to the notion of right quality amended by a calculation framework. Thus, we define Right Software and Systems Quality (RiSSQ) as

> ... the degree to which the ICT landscape as a whole or a particular ICT product as part of it satisfies the stated and implied needs of its various stakeholders under the frame conditions of a given budget, a given timeframe and a given risk level.

The RiSSQ notion guarantees that affordability in that budget, risk and time are associated with the validity of quality (cf. Fig. 3.8).

The timeframe is the amount of time after which the enterprise would like to have a certain level of quality of its ICT landscape or parts of it. Maybe this can be differentiated for various domains and their corresponding ICT systems, but at first

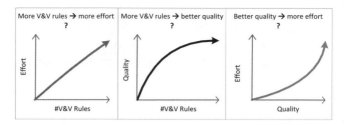

Fig. 3.6 Better quality implications?

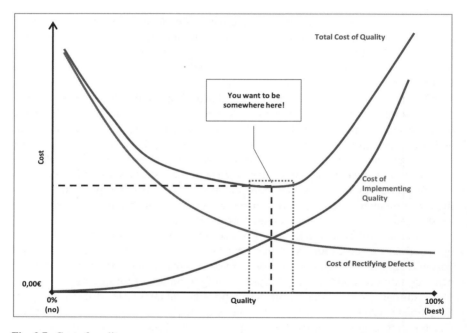

Fig. 3.7 Cost of quality

instance it is the whole ICT systems landscape. Note that this does not include process quality. To determine the timeframe, the stakeholder's opinions must be sought. Basically, risk is the probability of damage leading to an index multiplied by the resulting cost when it happens. Risk is thus an expectation value and is used to compare risk levels. Risk management generally provides means for risk avoidance, risk reduction, risk dissemination, risk transfer, risk insurance and risk acceptance. We can use such methods, procedures and tools to find out the corresponding risk level. All these activities need a certain amount of money to be conducted; quality, too, is not free. Therefore, some budget is needed for analytical as well as constructive assurance of quality.

Insofar as we have reached right quality within the triangle, we also have quality that is affordable. Unfortunately, this does not mean that we have also optimised the

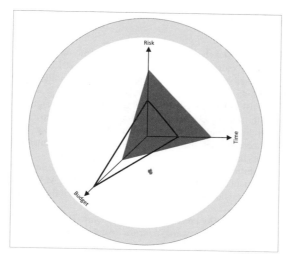

Fig. 3.8 RiSSQ triangle

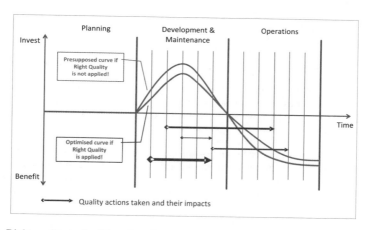

Fig. 3.9 Right quality in the lifecycle reduces overall investments

relation between risk, budget and time. Optimisation of this relation, or in other words an optimised quality investment depends on a number of other factors. Nevertheless, the benefit of quality management and quality assurance is given by the transparency reached and the difference between the damage costs caused by the risks and the costs of quality management and quality assurance. The effect of such an approach is illustrated in Fig. 3.9.

Usually we have a cost curve for ICT products like the blue one. If quality actions are taken in early phases just in development, we would then expect their impacts not only to be seen in this phase but in operations too. We could expect the green curve. For a detailed discussion on investment in right quality we refer to Chap. 4 on portfolio management and Chap. 7.

References and Links

Bourne L (2012) The value of stakeholder management. http://mosaicprojects.wordpress.com/2012/08/13/the-value-of-stakeholder-management/. Posted 13 Aug 2012. Retrieved 23 Nov 2013

Chen L, Ali Babar M, Nuseibeh B (2013) Characterizing architecturally significant requirements. IEEE Softw 30(2):38–45

Clements P, Bass L (2010) Relating business goals to architecturally significant requirements for software systems. http://www.sei.cmu.edu/reports/10tn018.pdf. Retrieved 18 Nov 2013

Clerc V (2009) Do architectural knowledge product measures make a difference in GSD?. In: ICGSE '09 proceedings of the 2009 fourth IEEE international conference on global software engineering. IEEE Computer Society, Washington, DC

Chrissis M, Konrad M, Shrum S (2011) CMMI for development: guidelines for process integration and product improvement, 3rd edn. Pearson Education, Boston, MA

DPE (2013). http://www.digitalpreservationeurope.eu/what-is-digital-preservation/#97. Retrieved 20 Nov 2013

Feigenbaum A (1991) Total quality control, 3rd edn. McGraw-Hill, New York, NY

Grady R, Caswell D (1987) Software metrics: establishing a company-wide program. Prentice Hall, Englewood Cliffs, NJ

Hauser J, Clausing D (1988) The house of quality. Harv Bus Rev (May–June): 63–73

ISO/IEC 15504-1 (2004) Information technology—process assessment—part 1: concepts and vocabulary. International Organization for Standardization (ISO), Geneva

ISO/IEC 15504-4 (2004) Information technology—process assessment—part 4: guidance on use for process improvement and process capability determination. International Organization for Standardization (ISO), Geneva

ISO/IEC 15504-5 (2012) Information technology–process assessment—part 5: an exemplar software life cycle process assessment model. International Organization for Standardization (ISO), Geneva

ISO/IEC 15504-7 (2008) Information technology—process assessment—part 7: assessment of organizational maturity. International Organization for Standardization (ISO), Geneva

ISO/IEC 25010 (2011) Systems and software engineering—systems and software quality requirements and evaluation (SQuaRE)—system and software quality models. International Organization for Standardization (ISO), Geneva

ISO/IEC 25012 (2008) Software engineering—software product quality requirements and evaluation (SQuaRE)—data quality model. International Organization for Standardization (ISO), Geneva

Kan S (1995) Metrics and models in software quality engineering. Addison-Wesley, Boston, MA

Kano (2013). http://upload.wikimedia.org/wikipedia/commons/6/68/Kano_model_showing_transition_over_time.png. Retrieved 21 Nov 2013

Kano N, Seraku N, Takahashi F, Tsuji S (1984) Attractive quality and must-be quality. J Jpn Soc Qual Cont 14(2):39–48

Kazman R, Klein M, Clements P (2000) ATAM: method for architecture evaluation. Carnegie Mellon University, Software Engineering Institute, Pittsburgh, PA

Lehman M, Belady L (1985) Program evolution—processes of software change. Academic, London

Rupp C, die SOPHISTen (2007) Requirements-Engineering und Management: Professionelle, interative Anforderungsanalyse für die Praxis. Carl Hanser Verlag, München Wien

Sauerwein E, Bailom F, Matzler K, Hinterhuber H (1996) The Kano model: how to delight your customers. In: Preprints volume I of the IX. International working seminar on production economics, Innsbruck/Igls, Austria, 19–23 Feb 1996, pp 313–327

Schmitz P, Bons H, van Megen R (1982) Software-Qualitätssicherung, Testen im Software-Lebenszyklus. Springer Vieweg Verlag, Wiesbaden

Simon F, Seng O, Mohaupt T (2006) Code-quality-management—Technische Qualität industrieller Softwaresysteme transparent und vergleichbar gemacht. dpunkt.verlag, Heidelberg

Simon F, Simon D (2010) Qualitäts-Risiko-Management—Ganzheitliche IT Projektsteuerung. Logos Verlag, Berlin

Wagner S (2013) Software product quality control. Springer, Berlin

Chapter 4
How Can We Establish Right Quality for an Enterprise?

In 2012, ISACA published results from a survey of over 3,700 global business and IT professionals and members of ISACA (2012b). More than 40 % worked in organisations in the finance, banking, insurance, government and military sectors. One surprising result was that more than 50 % of respondents indicated "business management's level of involvement in the governance of enterprise IT is not very high".

In our view, it is time in the ICT world to take a product-oriented rather than a purely project-oriented view. ICT systems are products, so there are two important issues to consider: ensuring it is the right product and guaranteeing that the product has the right quality. Clear goals from management are needed which set the scope and freedom for actions but also for quality characteristics. "It is not difficult to do things but it is difficult to provide an environment where things are dispensable" (freely adapted from Constantin Brancusi, 1876–1957).

In this chapter we will discuss our concept of quality governance and quality management aimed at all three layers of an enterprise, i.e. the strategic, the tactical and the operational layer. These disciplines must be aligned with stakeholders' demands. Changes in behaviour and requirements of the stakeholders have impact on right quality. First a critical acclaim of actual ICT governance will be undertaken, followed by the discussion of our holistic approach to enterprise ICT quality. Subsequent sections will discuss each enterprise layer individually.

4.1 A Critical Acclaim of ICT Governance

For many years ISACA and the IT Governance Institute have defined and distributed a reference model and framework called COBIT in the field of enterprise and IT governance. COBIT originated on behalf of internal and external accountants and auditors. The latest version, COBIT5, presents five key principles for governance and management of enterprise IT (ISACA 2012a):

M. Wieczorek et al., *Systems and Software Quality*,
DOI 10.1007/978-3-642-39971-8_4, © Springer-Verlag Berlin Heidelberg 2014

1. **Meeting stakeholder needs**—Enterprises exist to create value for their stake-holders by maintaining a balance between the realisation of benefits and the optimisation of risk and use of resources;
2. **Covering the enterprise end-to-end**—Governance of enterprise IT should be an integral part of enterprise governance;
3. **Applying a single, integrated framework**—There are many IT-related standards and good practices, each providing guidance on a subset of IT activities. They should be aligned with other relevant standards and frameworks at a high level to serve as an overarching framework for governance and management of enterprise IT;
4. **Enabling a holistic approach**—Efficient and effective governance and management of enterprise IT require a holistic approach, taking into account several interacting components. A set of enablers are needed to support the implementation of a comprehensive governance and management system for enterprise IT. Enablers are broadly defined as anything that can help to achieve the objectives of the enterprise, e.g. principles, policies and frameworks, processes, organisational structures, culture, ethics and behaviour, information services, infrastructure and applications, people, skills and competencies;
5. **Separating governance from management**—A clear distinction should be made between governance and management. These two disciplines encompass different types of activities, require different organisational structures and serve different purposes.

Generally speaking, these five principles are of course true and valuable. Today, ICT is an integral part of the business of enterprises. It is no longer a question of aligning ICT to business but it is a question of having the right things at the right time at the right place. Is the investment in ICT complementary to the business strategy? Does the ICT strategy support the business strategy adequately? Are ICT operations aligned to business operations adequately?

Traditionally, value delivery of ICT means "on time, within budget, to the appropriate quality and delivering the anticipated returns to the business". This can be taken to mean delivering with increased competitive advantage, with reduced order fulfilment time (quicker delivery), with increased customer satisfaction, with reduced customer wait time, with increased productivity or with reduced customer attrition. Therefore, value delivery of ICT is a requirement for the business to effectively manage both the cost of investments and the return on investment. The balance will become predictable if a holistic quality approach is in place.

The business has to demonstrate enterprise-wide governance to its stakeholders, e.g. shareholders, customers and employees. Within ICT governance this encompasses technology risk, ensuring the most appropriate technology is deployed as part of the solution, and that information security and information security measures are deployed to ensure that data protection laws and guidelines are maintained within the solutions. Nearly all enterprises are totally dependent on their technology to succeed. ICT needs to ensure that the risks of both new and aging technologies do not compromise the business. Risks need to be transparent within the organisation and all risks should be mitigated, accepted or transferred but never neglected.

Resource management is about optimising use of knowledge as well as use of infrastructure to ensure maximum return. Responsibilities for the efficient procurement of ICT systems and services need to be defined, understood by all parties, and then effectively applied. There is also a need to ensure that appropriate methods and skills exist to manage and support ICT systems and services. This requires putting in place career planning for ICT personnel to ensure retention of existing skilled staff and introducing recruitment concepts for any additional resources required so that successful delivery can be achieved.

Measurement and reporting procedures to prove that processes and procedures, resources and products (ICT solutions) are performing as planned must be defined and deployed. Depending on the layer concerned, reporting to the board and executive management should be as simple as possible and should be easily understood. Implementation of ICT governance is essential to ensure ICT departments and suppliers are effectively controlled by best practice and by the application of necessary controls. The ICT governance framework described above is being adopted by many organisations that want a standard "Best Practice" approach to organising and managing ICT within the framework of an efficient business.

However, the recognised standard ICT governance framework, when implemented, does not guarantee business units are making the most of ICT investments. Nor does it guarantee that the results of ICT and business system integration are delivering the right quality of business processes. The improved performance levels within the overall business are the measure of the correct quality of business processes. This is mostly measured in financial terms but can also be measured in tangible terms by information delivered on improvement in market share, customer satisfaction levels and increased business efficiency. What we are missing here is a notion of right quality implemented directly as part of a holistic enterprise quality system or related to the risk model of an enterprise.

In their framework (ISACA 2012a), ISACA and the IT Governance Institute consider governance and management as different disciplines of an enterprise and define these as follows:

> "**Governance** ensures that stakeholder needs, conditions and options are evaluated to determine balanced, agreed-on enterprise objectives to be achieved; setting direction through prioritization and decision making; and monitoring performance and compliance against agreed-on direction and objectives. In most enterprises, overall governance is the responsibility of the board of directors under the leadership of the chairperson. Specific governance responsibilities may be delegated to special organisational structures at an appropriate level, particularly in larger, complex enterprises".

> "**Management** plans, builds, runs and monitors activities in alignment with the direction set by the governance body to achieve the enterprise objectives. In most enterprises, management is the responsibility of the executive management under the leadership of the chief".

These definitions also provide a good foundation for our purposes, but they need to be complemented in the direction of clear right quality issues. The notion of quality is—if at all—inherently given by words like "stakeholder needs", "objectives to be achieved" and "part of the enabler". As a consequence, the board of directors and executive management will measure the success of an enterprise by economic means only. We believe that an enterprise must be interested in sustainable business and, therefore, needs to embed quality at all layers in an enterprise enabled by a holistic enterprise quality approach. We need the right products, meaning the right functionality of ICT systems, but we also need the right quality of such products to enable business to do their job in the right way. We also need right processes, procedures and tools which support all the activities around development and maintenance of such products.

In 2012, ISACA published results from a survey of over 3,700 global business and ICT professionals and members of ISACA (2012b). More than 40 % worked in organisations in the finance, banking, insurance, government and military sectors. In summary, this survey reveals that:

1. 74 % of the respondents say their enterprise's executive team believe information and technology to be important to the delivery of the enterprise's strategy and vision;
2. 52 % say they do not have enough ICT staff;
3. Data leakage is among the top hot-button security challenges facing enterprises in the next 12 months;
4. 47 % of enterprises have incurred an unexpected cost due to an ICT-related problem or incident in the last year;
5. More than half of responding enterprises use a framework/standard for governance and management of enterprise ICT assets and services;
6. More than 50 % of respondents say business management's level of involvement in the governance of enterprise ICT is not high;
7. 44 % of enterprises expect increasing investments in ICT over the next 12 months if it contributes to business value;
8. 34 % of the respondents say that the greatest benefits from ICT investments are directed to improved customer service, while only 18 % see cost reduction as the greatest benefit;
9. 32 % of the enterprises ended or cancelled an ICT-related project before it completed its task;
10. In 33 % of the cancelled projects the reason was "not delivered as promised" and in 37 % "the business needs have changed".

From our quality perspective, six statements—1, 3, 4, 6, 9, 10—are interesting for quality issues. If we are to achieve better business quality and, most importantly, continuously improve business quality we need to look at ICT and business operations. A good business strategy is required to direct the business and this strategy should provide an additional way of directing and governing business quality. Affordable quality must be the driver of enterprise ICT, for which a holistic enterprise quality approach is needed comprising quality governance, quality management and quality engineering best practices. And this must be underpinned by an industrialisation process that brings an enterprise to increased productivity, as is the case in other industries where industrialised processes are already in place. Investments in ICT must be aligned with the requirements of the relevant stakeholders and their changing behaviour.

4.2 Our Approach to Enterprise-Wide ICT Quality

Regulatory rules and compliance requirements like BASEL II and III (BIS 2013) are fundamental for increasing the resilience of complete markets, especially in a globalised world (c.f. other international and national regulatory bodies, e.g. NARUC (2013) in the US). Enterprises have to implement such rules and requirements and have to adhere to them. Nowadays, these rules cannot be implemented efficiently without ICT, and ICT itself has become subject to these regulatory rules. So ICT has to guarantee a certain degree of freedom from risk and needs to have risk mitigation procedures in place (cf. Wieczorek et al. 2002). In other words, ICT has to ensure a certain degree of quality. This is exactly the link for our holistic approach to enterprise-wide ICT quality. We believe that our approach can contribute to this in an excellent way by means of quality governance, quality management and industrialised quality engineering. We also feel that it is time for ICT to take a product-oriented view on ICT rather than a purely project-oriented one. ICT systems, applications, etc. are products. There are two important issues to consider: the right products and the right quality of such products.

Clear goals from the top management are also needed to set the scope and freedom of actions and include quality characteristics. Consequently, the board of directors and executive management must be part of the overall planning, monitoring and controlling process for ICT products and their quality, otherwise alignment of business and ICT will be inappropriate. Sustainable business will not be possible without sustainable ICT. Therefore, ICT quality needs to be embedded at all layers of an enterprise. Missing ICT quality will lead to high risks for the success of an enterprise. Our holistic quality approach to enterprise ICT takes this into account (cf. Fig. 4.1). The key objects in our approach are the quality risk model at the strategic layer, the quality models and verification and validation assets at the tactical layer, and the quality requirements and verification and validation assets at the operational layer.

At first glance, the overall process for setting up such an approach is simple:

1. Strategic layer:

   (a) Define or update the quality risk model;
   (b) Define or update the quality governance approach from a strategic viewpoint;
   (c) Provide the quality risk model to the tactical layer.

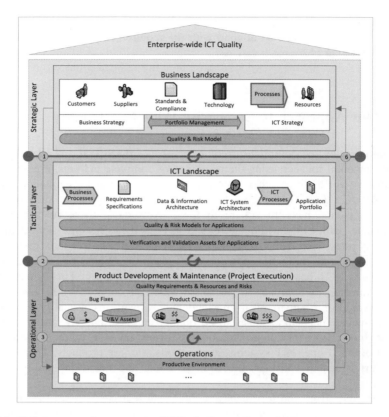

Fig. 4.1 Holistic approach to enterprise ICT including quality and risk

2. Tactical layer:

   (a) Define or update the quality models;
   (b) Define or update the quality governance approach from a tactical viewpoint;
   (c) Define or maintain the verification and validation assets;
   (d) As soon as a strategic development project is set up, provide the quality models as well as all the verification and validation assets to the project;
   (e) Provide aggregated quality feedback to the strategic layer.

3. Operational layer:

   a. Define the detailed quality requirements;
   b. Ensure that the detailed quality requirements are in accordance with the quality models;
   c. Adjust the verification and validation assets;
   d. Conduct verification and validation using the respective assets;
   e. Provide aggregated quality feedback to the tactical layer;

What remains to be defined is some kind of connection between quality issues at the three layers of an enterprise. This is given in our approach by the management disciplines of quality governance, quality management and portfolio management. They implement the feedback loop represented in Fig. 4.1 by the numbers 1–6.

Portfolio management defines the link between business and ICT to get the right investments for ICT products and their quality. Quality governance sets direction through prioritisation and decision making, monitoring performance and compliance against agreed-on objectives. Quality management takes care that all activities for ensuring the right quality of ICT products and processes are planned, built, run and monitored in alignment with the direction set by the governance body to achieve the enterprise objectives. We will discuss the relationship between portfolio management and all other quality issues in more detail in the subsequent sections of this chapter.

Having such an enterprise-wide ICT quality approach in place, it is then worthwhile to think about a framework for the implementation process. A detailed discussion is provided in Chap. 5. But the steps are now well-prepared. Software development for a particular product, system or for the whole landscape or replacement of business domain software can now be driven by the right quality as defined at the various layers of an enterprise. Whether it is outsourced or internally driven no longer matters, because services can be defined that are executable in an appropriate way, depending on the frame conditions of the enterprise. Quality issues are completely predefined by means of the quality models and the verification and validation assets at the tactical layer. It is also important to mention that the responsibility for those artefacts is completely associated to the respective role in the enterprise. The quality assets at the tactical layer can be given to the responsible unit at the operational layer and used for validation and verification.

4.3 Portfolio Management and Business Landscape

Within the business landscape at the strategic layer there is dynamic interaction between customers, suppliers, and the enterprise's various technologies, processes, resources, standards, and compliance rules. Portfolio management has a broader reach than project management, in the sense that project management addresses the efficiencies of delivering scope based on defined timelines, budget allocations and resources, while portfolio management employs standardised processes that lead to enhanced visibility into the entire business investment plan. Ultimately, these consistencies support the decision-making process to properly plan and govern key investments based on their value to the organisation (cf. Fig. 4.2).

How can we convert strategies into projects or, alternatively, what do projects mean for business strategies? In Chap. 2 (Sect. 2.5), we emphasised that organisational competencies in portfolio and execution excellence drive successful implementation of business strategies. So every enterprise that needs to introduce products or services has to undergo a project phase to deliver the tangible product,

Fig. 4.2   Business landscape and the quality risk model

like an ICT product. Strategic planning is the systematic and formalised effort of a company to establish basic purposes, objectives, policies, and business strategies. Once completed, detailed plans can be developed to implement those policies and strategies. The enterprise systematically identifies opportunities and threats in combination with other relevant data. It makes decisions that exploit those opportunities and it eliminates or minimises the risks. The strategic planning process links long-term goals, medium-term options, and short-term budgets with programme plans.

By forcing the setting of objectives, future opportunities and risks are revealed and clarified. The process of distilling long and medium-term goals into short-term programme plans turns goals into actionable and manageable steps. Additionally, this exercise creates the foundation for quality and performance measurement as leading indicators. These actionable and manageable steps with quality and performance measurements are the projects and programmes that form the "language of work" where the strategies are converted into reality plans.

The strategic planning and project selection process is continuous. The process must be flexible and adaptable to internal and external changes to enable the organisation to take advantage of new knowledge about the changing environment. A portfolio management process addresses the alignment of projects and programmes to business strategy and to ICT strategy, evaluates the value performance or business benefits as a business case and supports investment decisions though prioritisation and optimisation of the initiatives using the strategic value defined. The portfolio process aligns the projects and programmes to the ICT strategy so that executives know how their project and programme investments stack up against the strategic goals and directions. The diagram in Fig. 4.3 schematically shows the strategic alignment of the objectives to the business portfolio and the programmes and projects that they support. The portfolio management process uses strategic drivers and an analytical hierarchy framework to align the strategy with the projects and programmes.

Portfolio management is an integrated, continuous process of identifying, prioritising, and managing a portfolio of projects in alignment with key performance metrics and strategic business objectives. An integrated portfolio management helps an organisation's process of making and managing project investment decisions to

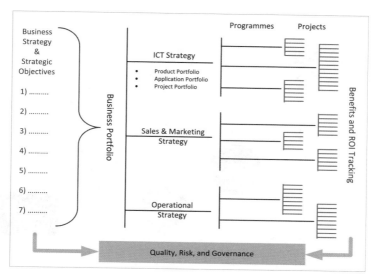

Fig. 4.3 Strategic alignment for delivery maximisation

maximise business benefit at a certain level of risk given certain constraints. The diagram in Fig. 4.4 shows an integrated portfolio management framework.

So portfolio management is not strategic management or strategy development. Corporate direction and departure from strategy are determined outside the remit of portfolio management, although the input from the ongoing information on the strategic goals and benefits generated by existing projects and programmes influence the strategy output (Rajegopal 2013).

Resilience and robustness is the ability of (business and ICT) processes, organisations, and technical systems to continue business and to protect their substance effectively from damage in the event of disruptions and incidents. Generally speaking, it is the ability to survive in case of trouble. Different strategies, methods and tools are well-known from risk management. Examples are:

- Awareness raising and qualification of staff;
- Early warning systems;
- Business continuity and fall-back mechanisms;
- Fault tolerance mechanisms;
- Redundancy in technical resources such as buffers and storage;
- Backup data and computer centre.

To achieve resilience and robustness it is necessary to have full transparency about the risk level for all business and ICT relevant objects. So the most important prerequisite for controlling and mitigating risks is being acutely aware of the risks. From a quality perspective this means that full transparency is needed for all ICT relevant objects and their quality. Therefore, the quality-relevant objects of the

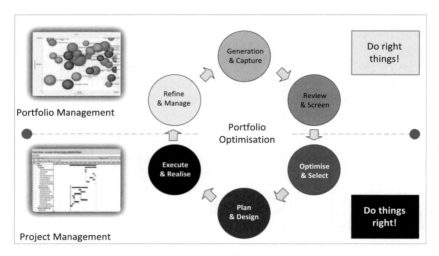

Fig. 4.4 Integrated portfolio management framework

business landscape in our approach are at least the customers, suppliers, staff, compliance rules, technology and all the processes of the enterprise (cf. Fig. 4.2).

Processes also represent the daily business roles in the workplace for all the people across the enterprise. Apart from the right business products, efficient and effective business processes are the key to an enterprise's success. It is obvious that such processes need to adhere to quality requirements which can be measured and monitored during the existence of that business. An ICT system as a whole needs to satisfy all these properties and must be constructed in the right way to support business efficiently and effectively through those processes. Additionally, resilience and robustness of business processes require various capabilities such as crisis management and business continuity management (cf. Wieczorek et al. 2002).

From a quality and risk perspective, the following actions have to be taken to evaluate the impact of changes in the business environment or in the business process portfolio:

- Analyse changes in markets and customers;
- Analyse changes in business products;
- Analyse changes in the whole process portfolio;
- Analyse current business and ICT risks;
- Analyse business and ICT risks coming from missing process and product quality in the past;
- Define or update the quality risk model on the basis of analysis results;
- Ensure that the quality governance structure is right.

Achieving strategy through effective execution is critical. An execution strategy is a discipline and delivery mechanism that involves both art and science to ensure that the stated benefits in the business case for an initiative are realised to improve the business's competitive advantage. Execution has to be part of a company's strategy and goals. It is the missing link between aspirations and results. A focused, agile and responsive approach to execution is key to ensuring business requirements and compliance mandates are delivered in accordance with expectations and benefits.

A well designed and deployed portfolio management process coordinates the prioritised delivery of corporate strategies through the execution of projects. You will realise that the project portfolio management process has been well accepted and established within the ICT functions of many industries as ICT gains greater recognition at board level. Properly executed portfolio management helps to overcome the root causes of portfolio failure. Once established, portfolio management addresses three fundamental questions:

• Are we doing the right projects?
• Are we confident that the projects we have chosen will be delivered well and meet their goals?
• For the projects we have completed, are we consciously changing how the organisation operates in order to realise the value we expected?

These are obviously fundamental, yet simple questions. Portfolio management also goes deeper to answer more complex questions like:

• How do we know we are doing the right projects?
• What criteria do we apply?
• What judgments do we make?
• Right projects as compared to what?

Once established and operational, portfolio management, amended by the enterprise-specific quality and risk models (cf. Fig. 4.1), provides:

• **Maximum value**—An optimised portfolio to achieve maximum strategic value and financial ROI under any given constraints;
• **Improved visibility**—A shared understanding of what the organisation is doing and why; objective, fact-based, less political decision making; ongoing insight into the status of initiatives and their joint impact on the strategic goals;
• **Improved effectiveness**—Ongoing evidence of project performance, benefits realisation and achievement of organisational change;
• **Reduced execution risk**—Upfront investigation of investment risk, launch of project with a high likelihood of success and allocation of resources to prioritised initiatives; partnered with comprehensive monitoring and control at portfolio level, projects are provided with the best possible environment for successful delivery.

Remember from previous chapters that coincidental quality is free, as it is built into the product by product development and maintenance. But if we ask product development what the risk level is, it is most often not easy to get insightful and comprehensive answers. It is therefore necessary to define other ways to get transparency. As discussed in Chap. 3, quality cannot be defined in absolute terms. It is always a certain level of quality and a certain level of risk which can be planned and reached. Both disciplines require effort. In the case of quality it is an

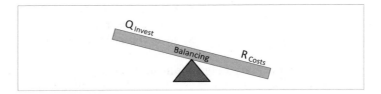

Fig. 4.5 Low quality leads to high risk

investment in the future to mitigate disruptions, and in the case of risk it is the costs when risks become losses. Risks can only be handled if they are known. Therefore, investing insufficiently in quality will lead to substantial costs afterwards. The goal is to balance investments for quality and costs for damages (cf. Fig. 4.5). For a detailed discussion we refer to Chap. 7.

4.4 Application Portfolio and ICT Landscape

The ICT landscape is moulded on the needs of the business and implements the business process portfolio. The risk- and quality-relevant objects of the ICT landscape are usually the various ICT products, business processes and requirements, data and information architecture, the ICT system architecture and last but not least, the ICT processes. ICT products and processes of right quality are therefore key to enterprise success. It is obvious that such products have to adhere to quality requirements which can be measured and monitored during the existence of their lifecycle and not only at the end of a project. Two things are necessary at the tactical layer of an enterprise to guarantee sustainable quality during the lifecycle: the quality models and the assets for verification and validation of the corresponding applications and business processes (cf. Fig. 4.6).

Application portfolio management complements the complex role of the ICT landscape. APM provides key information on the ICT landscape and answers questions such as "can yesterday's applications meet tomorrow's needs?" There is increasing pressure from ICT executives to cut costs, reduce inefficiencies, and to foster agility in systems. Enterprises invest more than 70 % of their budgets purely on maintaining their existing ICT asset investments. This shows that there is a clear and present broken link between strategic business objectives and "keeping the lights on" in the ICT landscape.

By using an application portfolio management approach, ICT decision makers can gain transparency about the application's impact that resides in the enterprise and which, if there is no clear application management strategy in place, hampers the enterprise's business. APM is a management framework for ICT decision makers to work within. APM defines a portfolio of application assets that provides visibility into the enterprise that we would not have without it. Application portfolio management and project portfolio management are very closely related activities.

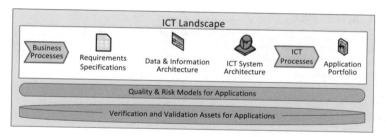

Fig. 4.6 ICT landscape, quality models and verification and validation assets

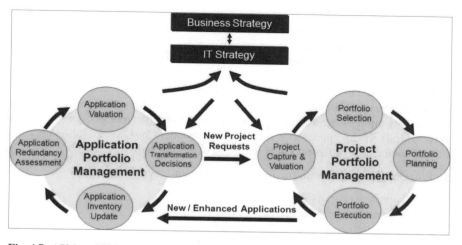

Fig. 4.7 APM vs. PPM

Sometimes there is confusion between the two. Although PPM and APM are very similar, they are also different as shown in Fig. 4.7.

A comparison of application portfolio management and project portfolio management is provided in Table 4.1.

The application portfolio management approach depicted in Fig. 4.6 is amended by the risk and quality models for applications and the related V&V assets. The quality and risk models at the tactical layer have to conform to the directives coming from the strategic layer by means of the quality risk model. The quality characteristics are then defined for the quality-relevant objects mentioned above. They are measured, monitored and last but least, improved. Usually such objects are collected in an object list so that every time questions arise about objects and their quality, these object lists can be applied. The advantage of such lists is that they allow us to point to the relevant issues. It is not about processes that are sometimes too complex, it is not about poor documentation that is not needed by anyone, and it is not about politics, which is the most significant source of irritation in enterprises and projects. A case in point is the old Y2K problem. All these objects

Table 4.1 APM vs. PPM

APM – focuses on the Application Architectures	PPM – focuses on Project Characteristics
• application-centric	• primarily project-driven
• takes non-tangible aspects into account, e.g. staff skills and education	• links to project resources
	• focuses on investments in the portfolio
• dependencies of applications	• ROI of programmes and projects
• links costs between applications	
• takes into account architecture, infrastructure, platforms, frameworks	
• supports IT governance holistically	

and object lists had been generated for transparency. Regrettably, all this work, which could have served as a good foundation for many enterprises, disappeared into dark holes and most often could not be reused afterwards.

A good approximation for the quality models at the tactical layer is given by the models discussed in Chap. 3. Which objects and which models are to be taken will be part of a quality initiative to implement our approach. But we believe that at least two quality models are required at this layer: a suitable process quality model (ProcQMod) and an appropriate system quality model (SysQMod). Remember the key characteristics of the two models as discussed in Chap. 3.

1. ProcQMod together with the following capability levels:

   – Incomplete process—capability level 0;
   – Performed process—capability level 1;
   – Managed process—capability level 2;
   – Established process—capability level 3;
   – Predictable process—capability level 4;
   – Optimising process—capability level 5.

2. SysQMod together with the following characteristics:

   – Functional completeness;
   – Functional correctness;
   – Functional appropriateness;
   – Usefulness;
   – Trust;
   – Pleasure;
   – Comfort;
   – Manageability (by release management).

From a quality perspective, the following actions have to be taken to evaluate the impact of changes in the ICT landscape of a particular enterprise:

• Implement the quality strategy defined at the strategic layer or improve the implementation;
• Evaluate the detailed quality characteristics;

- Define the tactical quality model (possibly sub-divided into ProcQMod and SysQMod);
- Define and implement or improve, monitor and control the quality infrastructure;
- Establish or maintain the verification and validation assets for the systems of the ICT landscape;
- Establish or maintain the verification and validation assets for all business processes of the business process portfolio.

Although not as a complete list, the following questions may help in defining the necessary quality and risk issues of the ICT landscape:

- Which business processes have changed?
- What is the impact of a business process on other business processes?
- What requirements have changed; business requirements or quality requirements?
- Is the degree of detail of quality requirements acceptable, i.e. are the quality requirements verifiable?
- Have compliance rules changed?
- Will technology or platforms change?
- Will staff change in quality or quantity?
- Which systems have changed or need to be modified?
- What is the impact of system changes on other systems and interfaces?
- Which projects have been set up?
- What impact do projects have on enterprise ICT?
- What impact do projects have on business processes, systems and other projects?

4.5   Project Execution

The road to project execution and success is often littered with conflict resulting from disagreement among stakeholders. Programme leaders must work with incomplete or inaccurate information, and there is often ambiguity or lack of a clear definition of success in key programme elements. Some teams and team leaders appear to thrive under such conditions of conflict, uncertainty, and ambiguity, while others seem paralysed by indecision.

We believe that effective project teams share four common characteristics. First, they can articulate the common goals that they are committed to achieve. Second, they acknowledge a mutual dependency on and demonstrate trust for one another. To accomplish this, there must be an understanding of and respect for team roles and responsibilities. Third, the team must accept a common set of behavioural norms—a common code of conduct. Fourth, they must accept the reward system that they will share.

As projects grow increasingly complex, project leaders are forced to rely on teams composed of highly skilled "knowledge workers." Since knowledge workers often resist close management, the centralised, command and control project management models have given way to loose, networked models where experts leverage their intellectual capital in support of primary project goals. Of course, these loose networks are not without challenges.

Technically challenging environments nearly always foster conflict among team members. In itself, conflict is not unhealthy. Quite the contrary—conflict, which frequently manifests as disagreement—is often a necessary precondition for group progress. Conflict can be an indication that the group is comfortable with open debate. However, conflict must be managed effectively so it is a source of power and not a de-motivating element. Nothing can derail a project faster than a breakdown in teamwork resulting from unmanaged conflicts.

By their very nature, complex projects almost always involve a high degree of uncertainty. Project leaders and team members must function with incomplete, inaccurate, or unknown information. This uncertainty can result in "second guessing" within the project team and other project stakeholders. Uncertainty in today's complex world must be acknowledged and accepted as an unavoidable condition.

Our crystal balls are not perfect. Consequently, frequent and open communication is absolutely essential to keep the team—and stakeholders—focused on the ultimate project objective. Weekly status reports, flash reports, frequent emails, and simply talking to one another on a regular basis can help keep uncertainty under control and mitigate its damaging effects on teamwork.

Ambiguity is another characteristic of complex projects that must be addressed by the team. More often than not, confusion surrounds key project elements or objectives. Even worse, ambiguity sometimes results from conflicting definitions of words. We recently worked with a large project team in a multi-national corporation where the team members kept arguing about the project "scope." Interestingly enough, when we pressed for their definition of "scope," we found that they were arguing over eight very different definitions!

The project team can mitigate ambiguity by taking the time to establish—and publish—a common set of terminology to serve as a team reference. There are published systems management dictionaries that can serve the same purpose. Other tools that can reduce ambiguity include: a highly visible status board containing project goals, the plan, and progress relative to the plan, frequent communications meetings, and frequent, informal dialogue among the project team members.

The operational layer as indicated in Fig. 4.1 above makes a distinction between product development and maintenance on the one hand and operations on the other hand. To begin with, we will focus on project execution (cf. Fig. 4.8).

Due to the volume and complexity of necessary modifications of the corresponding ICT product, in this section we have differentiated this part of operations into three sub-areas:

- Bug fixes;
- ICT product changes, including enhancements;
- New ICT products.

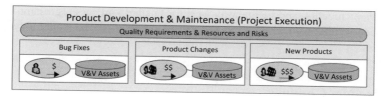

Fig. 4.8 Product development & maintenance, quality requirements and V&V assets

There are many quality engineering methods, procedures and tools that have to be applied according to the quality requirements and artefacts. Quality engineering usually comprises constructive and analytical methods that can be broken down further into static and dynamic ones. Static methods are usually applied for requirements, architecture and code analyses. Dynamic methods assume that running code is available and can be tested. Most of them are tool-based. See Appendix A for a sample overview of methods. For further reading we refer to e.g. ISO/IEC/IEEE 29119-1 (2013), ISO/IEC/IEEE 29119-2 (2013), ISO/IEC/IEEE 29119-3 (2013), Spillner and Linz (2005), Liggesmeyer (2002) and Koomen et al. (2008).

Bug Fixes

Bug fixes, or hot fixes, refer to production issues and issue management and imply system changes in current production releases of applications. A production issue prevents the application or execution of necessary business and system processes or represents an unwanted process or system behaviour, e.g. erroneous results, bad performance, etc. A bug fix will be implemented because of defects that were not identified within the development or maintenance project but came up during production. Examples of such non-identified defects are:

- Programming errors;
- Designing errors (e.g. wrong design of a technical solution to implement requirements); and
- Business requirement errors (e.g. wrong specification or missing requirement).

For each production issue there is an explicit analysis and decision on criticality to place a bug fix order immediately or to place that order as a system defect or change request for the next system release (e.g. a work-around can be put into place). An immediate bug fix allows less than a day or only a few days from order to production. Development but also quality assurance has to be executed within that short timeframe. The following actions have to be taken from a quality perspective:

- Search or define verification and validation assets to cover process scenarios that caused production issues and execute them;
- Apply verification and validation assets for system regression testing;

- Apply verification and validation assets for business process regression testing;
- Provide feedback on verification and validation assets to the tactical layer.

ICT Product Changes

Change requests refer to existing systems or applications and specify a new business or a new system requirement that has to be implemented by a planned project. It will be defined by portfolio management and change management processes. A change request can reference business processes, system processes or special system components and define functional and non-functional requirements. The following actions have to be taken from a quality perspective:

- Maintain the verification and validation assets of systems or define new ones;
- Maintain the verification and validation assets of business processes or define new ones;
- Apply verification and validation assets for system regression testing;
- Apply verification and validation assets for business process regression testing;
- Return verification and validation assets to the tactical layer;
- Verify and validate the particular artefacts;
- Verify the ICT landscape as a whole.

New Products

New products provide new business processes or add new functionality to current processes or replace current systems or applications, e.g. by introducing standard packages. New products are defined by portfolio management. The specification of new products includes all the functional and non-functional business requirements or detailed delta requirements in case of introducing standard packages. The following actions have to be taken from a quality perspective:

- Maintain the system V&V assets;
- Maintain the business process V&V assets;
- Define system V&V assets for the new product;
- Define business process V&V assets for the new product;
- Apply verification and validation assets for system regression testing;
- Apply verification and validation assets for business process regression testing;
- Return new verification and validation assets to the tactical layer;
- Validate and verify the particular artefacts of the new product;
- Verify the resulting ICT system(s); and
- Verify the ICT landscape as a whole.

Fig. 4.9 Production environment including quality monitoring

4.6   Operations

Remember from Fig. 4.1 above that the operational layer makes a distinction between product development and maintenance on the one hand and operations on the other hand. Operations (cf. Fig. 4.9) is concerned with all issues of running the ICT processes, including ICT service management, business continuity management, and first and second level support. Operations is therefore a strong source of improvement suggestions at the tactical and strategic layers. But Operations also needs information on risks coming from changes in the ICT landscape and the corresponding projects. As discussed in Wieczorek et al. (2002) and especially in Schettler et al. (2002) and Wallmüller (2002) there is a strong interdependence between quality issues and operations.

During project execution, Operations is a user stakeholder along with business users. At the end of a project Operations takes over system responsibility and provides access and use of systems and system results to business users. Business users take responsibility for business processes, and Operations takes responsibility for systems and system infrastructure to provide technical processes to support business.

As a user stakeholder, Operations also specifies requirements, i.e. functional and non-functional requirements concerning:

- Special system components like batch management system;
- System integration with hardware and system software infrastructure (see portability and compatibility), different versions of and future infrastructure;
- System configuration (see procedures but also non-conflicting configuration of different systems and applications); and last but not least
- Concepts and solutions for first and second level support as well as training in and documentation of use of products.

Projects have to cover these requirements through development but also through verification and validation; in some cases Operations will take over project activities because of technical resources that are only accessible by Operations, or because several projects and their systems are being integrated into a final release.

In production, Operations is responsible for ongoing operations, i.e. operation of products that:

- Provide systems to users;
- Execute batch systems and provide business results;
- Support and coach users in product use;
- Monitor technical processes, identify production issues, solve these issues or coordinate issue solving, e.g. by system owners.

References and Links

BIS (2013) http://www.bis.org/index.htm. Retrieved 15 Nov 2013

ISACA (2012a) COBIT 5—a business framework for the governance and management of enterprise IT. ISACA, Rolling Meadows, Illinois

ISACA (2012b) Governance of enterprise IT (GEIT) survey—global edition. http://www.isaca.org/Pages/2012-Governance-of-Enterprise-IT-GEIT-Survey.aspx. Retrieved 11 Nov 2013

ISO/IEC/IEEE 29119-1 (2013) Software and systems engineering—software testing—part 1: concepts and definitions. International Organization for Standardization (ISO), Geneva

ISO/IEC/IEEE 29119-2 (2013) Software and systems engineering—software testing—part 2: test processes. International Organization for Standardization (ISO), Geneva

ISO/IEC/IEEE 29119-3 (2013) Software and systems engineering—software testing—part 3: test documentation. International Organization for Standardization (ISO), Geneva

Koomen T, van der Alst L, Broekman B, Vroon M (2008) TMap Next, Ein praktischer Leitfaden für ergebnisorientiertes Softwaretesten. dpunkt.verlag, Heidelberg

Liggesmeyer P (2002) Software-Qualität: Testen, Analysieren und Verifizieren von Software. Spektrum Akademischer Verlag, Heidelberg

NARUC (2013) http://www.naruc.org. Retrieved 15 Nov 2013

Rajegopal S (2013) Portfolio management—how to innovate and invest in successful projects. Palgrave Macmillan, Basingstoke, Hampshire

Schettler H, Wieczorek M, Philipp M (2002) Operational risks and business continuity: an essayistic overview. In: Wieczorek M, Naujoks U, Bartlett B (eds) Business continuity—IT risk management for international corporations. Springer, Berlin

Spillner A, Linz T (2005) Basiswissen Softwaretest. dpunkt.verlag, Heidelberg

Wallmüller E (2002) Rsik management for IT and software projects. In: Wieczorek M, Naujoks U, Bartlett B (eds) Business continuity—IT risk management for international corporations. Springer, Berlin

Wieczorek M, Naujoks U, Bartlett B (eds) (2002) Business continuity—IT risk management for international corporations. Springer, Berlin

Chapter 5
How Can We Implement a Framework for Right Quality?

To create a framework for right quality that enables full transparency about the quality of products and alignment of risks with the business needs of the enterprise means to implement a holistic and integrated quality approach. In our view, this approach must be both product and process oriented. Our framework for enabling right quality accompanies organisations on their journey from relying completely on people acting individually to a highly efficient and profitable Quality Services Factory characterised by an adequate degree of industrialisation of quality engineering.

The most suitable way of evaluating and improving organisations through industrialisation is to successively implement the five dimensions of our "Industrialised House of Quality". These dimensions are modularisation, standardisation, specialisation, automation and continuous improvement supported by quality management and quality governance. The order in which this is done should be considered thoroughly; otherwise it could lead to a revision of the complete quality engineering approach.

The highest leverage effect can be reached by generally following the sequence above, even if it is possible and sometimes necessary to work in parallel on selected issues of different dimensions for local improvements or to mitigate high priority risks. For example, automation of particular quality aspects is most efficient when modularisation and standardisation has already been implemented to a certain extent to avoid redundant work and maintenance. Additionally, this order gives a high degree of reuse of pre-existing components.

We will discuss our "House of Quality" in the following sections, where we will cover each dimension as well as each management discipline.

M. Wieczorek et al., *Systems and Software Quality*,
DOI 10.1007/978-3-642-39971-8_5, © Springer-Verlag Berlin Heidelberg 2014

5.1   Industrialisation of Quality Engineering

Ever-growing technical innovations in the ICT industry increasingly affect the way in which a service or product is planned, built, delivered, and consumed. The new way ICT understands itself is often called industrialisation. When we examine the history of other industries like production oriented sectors we see that they have already undergone significant changes from craftsmanship to an industrialised approach characterised by specialisation and division of labour across enterprises and between enterprises by outsourcing part of the work. ICT is taking the first steps on this road right now. Bear in mind that the goal of every industrialisation approach is reduction of costs per piece or reduction of overall product costs. Realising such a goal locally in an enterprise also provides an opportunity to use globalisation to further reduce costs. But this presupposes that an enterprise has already implemented a certain level of right quality before globalisation can be used effectively for software and systems development in general and for quality engineering in particular.

From a Chief Financial Officer's perspective cost reduction seems to be the ultimate goal for an enterprise, but not for the sake of complacency; it is always a question of balance. Balance between quality and risk, balance between investment and benefit, balance between short-term success and sustainability. The following pain points are prevalent:

- Flexibility of all processes;
- Effectiveness and efficiency of all processes;
- Productivity in development and maintenance;
- Forward-looking and trend-setting approaches.

Take the field of core banking solutions [cf. (Free and Wang 2013)], like SAP, Temenos or Avaloq. In (Avaloq 2013), for example, Avaloq claims to support the value chain of banks through various industrialised offers like standard software, application service providing (ASP), business process outsourcing (BPO) and banking hub. Again, their goal is cost reduction of core banking processes while not neglecting the efficiency of business processes.

A key factor driving industrialisation approaches is technology and its evolution over time. In this sense industrialisation is regarded as a management concept that allows for cost-effective manufacturing of products. From discussions about industrialisation, as in (Buxmann et al. 2008) and (Capgemini 2012), or definitions in Wikipedia (Wiki-Industrie 2013) and (Wiki-Industrialisation 2013), industrialisation in general can be defined in the strict sense as:

"... the process of development and implementation of industrial production types"

This definition, however, neglects the macro-economic meaning of industrialisation from one economic sector to the next.

As in other industries, the process of development and implementation of industrial production types, i.e. the process of industrialisation of quality

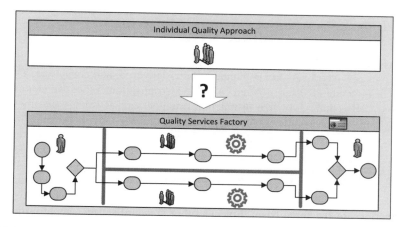

Fig. 5.1 From individual approach to Quality Services Factory

engineering, usually starts with one or a few people doing their job individually and producing a certain product. If the product is simple enough such a procedure works well. If the products become increasingly complex, more people are needed, more experts are needed and the procedures need standards. As soon as the production process or workflow is fully understood and suitable technology is available work flows or parts of them can be automated. Last but not least a factory approach can be applied to workflows. This is also true for quality engineering. Therefore we ask: what does "industrialising quality engineering" or setting up a "Quality Services Factory" means? This is illustrated schematically in Fig. 5.1.

In the first box—Individual Quality Approach—we find an unstructured workflow of people working independently on intermediate results and producing a final product. In the second box—Quality Services Factory—we find well-structured workflows where experts work together in teams and make use of tools. They run standard processes, produce intermediate results in conformity to these processes and achieve the intended final product. This is complemented by monitoring and controlling mechanisms to overcome deficiencies during execution.

During the last decade we have experienced another shortcoming with development and maintenance of software-based systems. Every time a project is set up by enterprise management due to bug fixes or change requests, it is because they are looking for the right quality assurance concept. Most often this is conceptually ambitious, but in reality it is time and cost intensive. What is done for a project to be able to use already existing experience and knowledge as well as validation and verification rules? Why do we most often have no test case portfolio that can be maintained and reused over time? Why is regression testing as time and cost consuming as the original testing? The main issue is that quality approaches are most often aligned with project needs and not with product and lifecycle needs. This is a good reason to examine our "industrialised House of Quality".

Of course, it is presupposed that quality assurance is an engineering discipline. Following (Buxmann et al. 2008), starting points for industrialisation of quality

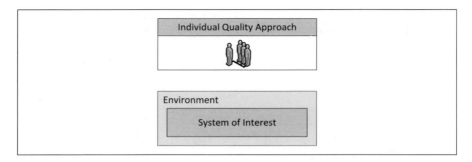

Fig. 5.2 Initial situation—IQA and system in environment

engineering are the three basic dimensions of standardisation, specialisation and automation. Without standardisation specialisation and automation will not effectively be applicable. But standardisation itself needs modularisation because if products or processes are not modularised it is not possible to efficiently standardise workflows or products. Consequently, modularisation, standardisation, specialisation and automation are valuable characteristics of industrialisation for the software industry as a whole but also for quality engineering. Specialisation also leads to division of labour and work-sharing so that efficient delivery and engagement models can be defined to reduce investments. What also is missing in (Buxmann et al. 2008) and needs to be adapted for our purposes is continuous improvement, as in (BITKOM 2010). This is needed because the environment of industrialised workflows may change or products are modified in a way that leads to inefficient processes if the procedures and tools are not adjusted.

The various steps on the way to our "industrialised House of Quality" are not completely independent of the type of software development processes and artefacts. Industrialisation in software development and quality engineering follows similar rules. In the best case, both flows are aligned but independently performed. As indicated above, industrialisation focuses on production types. So it will be necessary to discuss each dimension along with its impact on processes, products and people (cf. Chap. 2). Our initial picture is therefore Fig. 5.2, which shows that in IQA a process is not perceptible although people are working to produce a product, and that the product, i.e. system of interest, has no perceptible structure. This picture will subsequently be developed and completed for each dimension, in line with our holistic approach for enterprise ICT quality (cf. Chap. 4).

Obviously all actions taken in the five dimensions of industrialisation also have to be considered with respect to their impact on the three layers, i.e. strategic, tactical and operational. To this end we will develop, step by step, the different dimensions of industrialisation of quality engineering in the following sections. Not all these relationships are discussed in every subsection, but an overview is provided in Table 5.1.

As a practical running example of industrialisation of quality engineering, we will look at insurance software. Suppose we have software for the property

Table 5.1 Industrialisation dimensions related to enterprise layers

	Strategic Layer	Tactical Layer	Operational Layer
Modularisation	Business process landscape; Enterprise architecture; Organisational structure;	ICT product landscape; ICT Process landscape; Programme/Project landscape	System structure; Intermediate artefacts; Project-specific processes;
Standardisation	Specification of budgets, quality and risk; Reference standards, Industry standards; Development policies; Benchmarking framework;	Established enterprise standards; Methods, procedures, and tools; Organisational tailoring guidelines; Strategies ICT processes; Balancing quality and risk; Report and measurement database;	Tailored templates; Standardised products; Standardised processes; Standardised working environment; Programming standards; Style guides; Reusable system components;
Specialisation	Domain business; Standard software; Business process outsourcing; Organisational alignment; Sourcing decisions; Best of breed decisions;	Recruitment strategies; Qualification and education programmes; Division of work; Established workflow instructions; Different roles; Best of quality;	Recruitment; Education; Skill management; Dedicated teams; Quality gates;
Automation	Automation strategy to improve profitability, time to market, reproducibility, robust processes and quality;	Established regression concept; Automation architecture; Automation frameworks; Tooling and guidelines; Cost savings;	Implementation; Execution; Time savings;
Continuous Improvement	Quality governance; Product and quality ownership;	Project and product governance; Quality management; Quality models; Quality Intelligence Portal (KQI/KPI);	Audits and feedback loops; Lessons learned; Measuring and reporting; Monitoring and control of project goals; Improving quality of prediction (risk, budget, time).

insurance segment with functions for claims management, contract management and insured persons management. The V&V assets are, for example, test models, test cases, test data, manual test scripts but also test results and reports (cf. Fig. 5.3). The initial picture for our insurance example depicts the current stage of industrialisation in this book, i.e. monolithic processes, a monolithic product and monolithic V&V assets, and the target with a high degree of industrialisation.

In subsequent sections we assume that one of the goals of the corresponding enterprise is to develop the property insurance software in a way that allows it to be enhanced to other segments and transferred from one business unit to another and from one country to another.

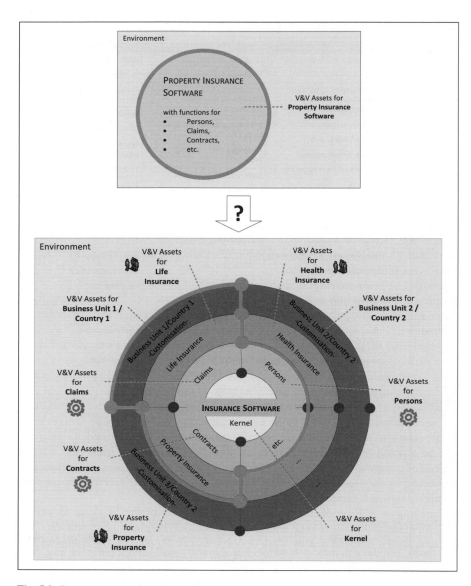

Fig. 5.3   Insurance example—V&V assets

5.2   Modularisation

The first step on our way to industrialisation of quality engineering is modularisation. Modularisation is the cornerstone for industrialisation. Generally speaking, the starting point is typically determined through monolithic workflows

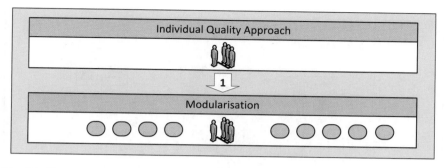

Fig. 5.4 First step—modularisation of QE workflow

defined over time, including responsibilities for their outcome. This works well as long as we are willing to accept that the people are completely self-organising their work and we totally rely on their capabilities, their experience, their foresight and their availability (cf. Fig. 5.4).

Instead of just requiring products and relying on the skills and expertise of the people during development or maintenance (first box), the workflows will follow an individual work breakdown structure (second box). In fact such structures include the required input and the expected output and the responsibilities. Bear in mind, however, that those structures should be moulded to individual or local conditions. Every time a product has to be manufactured no standardised procedure is available. Such modularised workflows are also accompanied by quality management, although information about intermediate steps is rarely available.

Modularisation is concerned with structuring and decomposing processes (cf. second box of Fig. 5.4). To be able to structure and decompose workflows it is necessary to structure and decompose products so that intermediate artefacts can be worked on in different steps (cf. Fig. 5.5). Remember from Fig. 4.1 that processes comprise all workflows in an enterprise, i.e. core business processes, ICT processes, management processes and supporting processes. Products, respectively, comprise business products as well as ICT products.

Looking at ICT products, we have all the artefacts of the lifecycle as part of development and maintenance and also operations. These comprise software and documentation but also quality-ware or V&V assets. It could be the complete ICT systems landscape but also a comprehensive enterprise architecture. As already mentioned, modularisation of products is determined by the goals and viewpoints of the stakeholders at the different layers of an enterprise. Note that modularisation may have standards available individually or locally, but they are not provided as a standard for the whole enterprise.

Some aspects to be considered in modularisation of quality engineering are:

- Testing as a whole and related test stages;
- Input and output artefacts;
- Software components like classes, programs and packages for test environments;

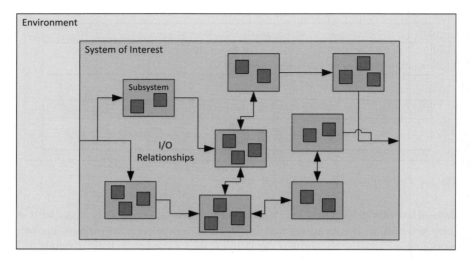

Fig. 5.5 Modularisation—sample product decomposition

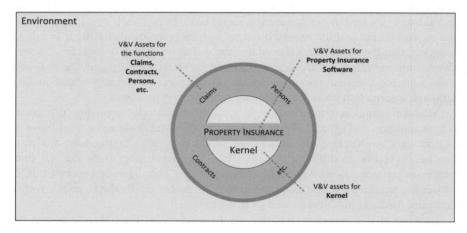

Fig. 5.6 Modularisation—insurance example

- Interfaces between different quality engineering processes;
- Interfaces between quality engineering and release and change management;
- Interfaces between quality engineering and development processes.

As a practical example for modularisation of quality-ware we will look at our insurance software. Suppose we have software for the property insurance segment with functions for claims management, contract management and insured person management. The V&V assets are, e.g. test cases, manual test scripts but also test results and reports. Then the picture we would like to start with our running example is provided in Fig. 5.6.

In this stage quality-ware should be moulded to the structure of the given product or parts of it. Modularisation of quality-ware in this example therefore means building V&V assets for the various layers and their components. Thus, we can differentiate for example between:

- V&V assets for kernel for the verification of modules and components;
- V&V assets for the various functions for claims, contracts, persons, etc. to verify all the functional and non-functional quality requirements; and
- V&V assets for the Property Insurance software as a whole to verify that the business processes can be performed with the right quality.

5.3 Standardisation

The second step in our method of industrialisation of quality engineering is standardisation. A prerequisite for standardisation is modularisation. Generally speaking, the starting point of standardisation is typically determined through decomposed workflows defined over time, including responsibilities given to individuals. This works well as long as we are willing to accept that every person or team is completely self-organising their modularized workflows and we totally rely on their capabilities, their experience, their foresight and their availability (cf. Fig. 5.7). This is similar to the initial situation in modularisation.

Instead of just requiring products and relying on the skills and expertise of the people during development or maintenance and their individual work breakdown structure (cf. second box in Fig. 5.7), the workflows will now follow standardised work breakdown structures (cf. third box in Fig. 5.7). The difference with modularisation is in fact that decomposition of workflows is predefined. Such structures include the required input and expected output and the overall responsibilities given to single persons or teams within the workflows. The standardised workflows are accompanied by quality management where information about intermediate steps will now be available.

Standardisation is concerned with ensuring that structured and decomposed processes are conducted throughout the enterprise or an autonomous organisational unit. Standardisation provides the opportunity to adjust the individual approaches from IQA—task, qualification, tools, etc.—to a common approach where each participant in the process has to accepts and follow its definition. This will avoid the invention of new workflows every time a new project or task is started and will reduce the probability of failing processes not achieving the defined goals.

Looking at ICT products, we have again all the artefacts of the lifecycle as part of development and maintenance and operations. It could be software and documentation but also quality-ware or V&V assets. It could also be the complete ICT systems landscape or the comprehensive enterprise architecture. Standardisation with respect to products assures the interchangeability and reusability of products; it supports product lines and variants and tries to eliminate redundancy where this makes sense. In contrast to modularisation, standardisation will not be possible

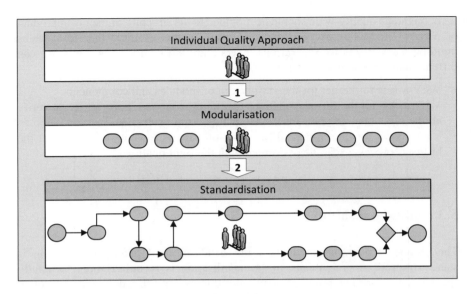

Fig. 5.7 Second step—standardisation of QE workflow

without strong, enterprise-wide support from the management. To benefit from standardisation it is essential that the standards are established beyond the boundaries of personal responsibilities and projects.

Many standards and quasi-standards are available for most of the relevant processes and artefacts. Examples of process models in development and maintenance are CMMI (Chrissis et al. 2011) and SPICE (ISO-15504 2011); in testing it is TestSPICE (TestSPICE-PAM 2012) and (TestSPICE-PRM 2012), TMMI (van Veenendaal and Wells 2012), ISTQB (Spillner et al. 2011) and TMap Next (Koomen et al. 2008); and in operations it is ITIL (ITIL 2011). Process models are mostly complemented by assessment models for evaluating and improving processes. Similarly, we find many standards for products and artefacts of the lifecycle. Examples in this field are WSDL (WSDL 2007) for defining technical interfaces between services; UML (UML 2011) for describing and modelling all the artefacts in software engineering; and TOGAF, NAF, Zachman Framework, SAGA (Schekkerman 2006) for describing and modelling architectures. Interfaces must use standards to the best possible extent. Standardisation, here, is the precondition for exchangeability and reusability of products, product components and processes. It is also a prerequisite for selecting new suppliers or replacing one supplier by another. Internal standards are valuable to harmonise and facilitate internal information exchange, but the adaptation of industry standards is preferred as they enable interchangeability within enterprises and across companies.

Standardisation of products is accompanied by component libraries giving easy access to standardised specific modules and components (cf. Fig. 5.8). Ideally, this is complemented by release and configuration management processes that control the usage and number of possible variants in an adequate and efficient way.

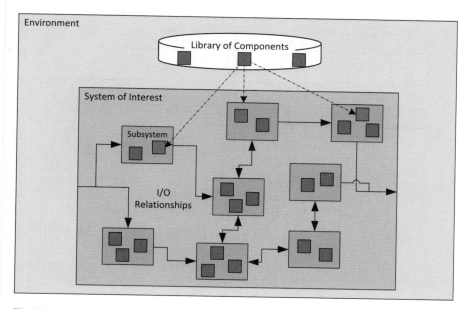

Fig. 5.8 Standardisation—sample product decomposition

Some aspects to be considered in standardisation of quality engineering are:

- Verification and validation as a whole;
- Appropriate process models together with related analysis and improvement models;
- Right quality of component libraries;
- Interfaces between different quality engineering processes;
- Interfaces between quality engineering and release and change management;
- Interfaces between quality engineering and development processes.

In Sect. 5.1 we started a practical example from the insurance field to discuss the various dimensions and their impact on quality engineering and the respective artefacts, the quality-ware. Standardisation now delivers the picture shown in Fig. 5.9. Note: we are not discussing other industrialisation dimensions here. From modularisation (cf. Fig. 5.6) we know the inner two circles comprising kernel functionality and functionality for claims, contracts and persons management. We have now added a further layer to indicate that the insurance software has to be implemented for different business units of an enterprise by means of customisation. This could be the case, for example, if a company incorporates another company.

Suppose that the V&V assets again consist of, for example, test models, test cases, test data, manual test scripts but also test results and reports. In standardisation it is the goal not only to define standards for quality engineering but also to provide standardised V&V assets to make the corresponding processes more efficient. This can be achieved for example through a standard test case portfolio and corresponding test scripts for functional testing of claims, contracts and persons

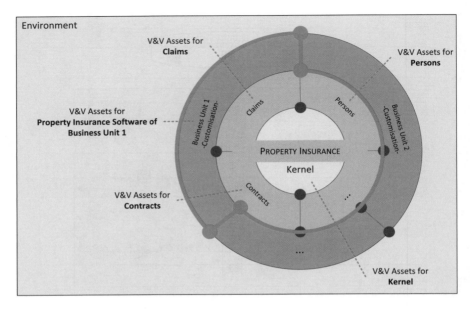

Fig. 5.9 Standardisation—insurance example

management. Such standard assets can also be applied to business process testing in case of the whole property insurance software for a particular business unit. These standardised V&V assets can subsequently be adapted to other environments, e.g. other business units. This makes verification for new business units most efficient and cost-effective.

Quality-ware is most often moulded to the structure of the given product or parts of it. Assume that we have libraries for the kernel, for claims management, for contract management, for persons management, etc. So we can differentiate for example between:

- V&V assets for kernel for the verification of modules, components and libraries;
- V&V assets for claims management;
- V&V assets for contracts management;
- V&V assets for persons management;
- V&V assets for the customisation of the property insurance software for a business unit.

5.4   Specialisation

The third step in our method of industrialisation of quality engineering is special-isation. Prerequisites for specialisation are modularisation and standardisation. Generally speaking, the starting point for specialisation is typically determined

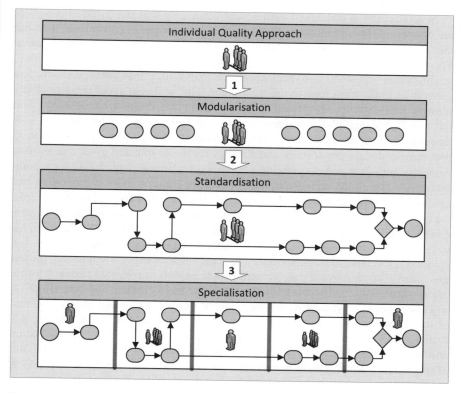

Fig. 5.10 Third step—specialisation of QE workflow

through the standardised, decomposed workflows, including responsibilities given to individuals or teams. This works well as long as we are willing to accept that every person is a generalist who is completely self-organising along the standardised workflows. Again we totally rely on the persons' capability, experience, foresight and availability (cf. Fig. 5.10). This is similar to the initial situation in standardisation.

Instead of just requiring standardised products and relying on the skills and expertise of generalists during development or maintenance and their standard work breakdown structure (third box in Fig. 5.10), the workflows will be structured such that experts for the respective part of the workflow perform the corresponding tasks (fourth box in Fig. 5.10). The difference with modularisation and standardisation is in fact that decomposition and structuring of workflows and products are now moulded to specialists instead of generalists. Such structures again include the required input and expected output and the responsibilities. The specialised and standardised workflows are also accompanied by quality management. Information about intermediate steps of the workflows and intermediate work products will also be available, as in standardisation.

Specialisation is concerned with ensuring not only that standardised processes are conducted throughout the enterprise or an autonomous organisational unit, but that the people have the right qualification for the tasks they have to perform. Specialisation provides the opportunity to adjust the generalist approaches—task, qualification, tools—to a hybrid approach that brings together specialists and generalists at the right time in the right place. This will also avoid wasting of key players' time and capacity. Based on this you can either improve by reducing effort through better qualified resources (people and technology) or by reducing cost through substitution of own resources by specialised suppliers. Specialisation in processes and tasks creates new possibilities for the people and gives rise to cross company activities and outsourcing concepts (cf. (Young et al. 2008) for a comprehensive discussion on outsourcing). Where we are used to have generalists like quality managers and test managers doing all the corresponding work in their role, we can now differentiate better in tasks and create new roles like process managers, quality managers and product managers in the field of enterprise ICT quality. In the field of quality engineering, new roles include test managers, test engineers, test architects, test designers, performance experts, security experts and testers for test execution. This will avoid unmotivated people as well as overpaid people because of over-qualification. The workflows will become more efficient and cost-effective.

Looking at ICT products, we have again all the artefacts of the lifecycle as part of development and maintenance and operations. It could be the complete ICT systems landscape but also a comprehensive enterprise-architecture. Specialisation ensures more flexibility and reusability of products because we can now make use of specialists' know-how and experience. Structures and decomposition of products is focused on specific aspects which often relate to software and quality engineering; it supports domain-specific product lines and variants, separates technical components from business specific components and tries to eliminate redundancy where this makes sense. In contrast to modularisation but like standardisation, specialisation is not possible without strong, enterprise-wide support from the management. To benefit from specialisation it is essential that the standards are established beyond the boundaries of personal responsibilities and projects. To realize the potential of this dimension it is necessary to know the skills and competencies required for relevant aspects to be covered by the organisation. It is again essential that the enterprise has an appropriate skills and qualification scheme.

Product specialisation is achieved by libraries of cross-domain components giving easy access to standardised modules and components from a technical and business viewpoint (cf. Fig. 5.11). Ideally, this is complemented by release and configuration management processes controlling the usage and number of possible variants in an adequate and efficient way.

Some aspects to be considered in specialisation of quality engineering are:

- Verification and validation as a whole;
- Standardised process models together with related analysis and improvement models;

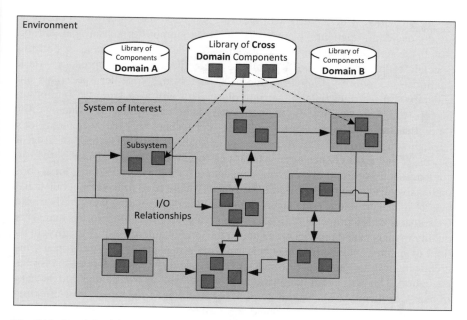

Fig. 5.11 Specialisation—sample product decomposition

- Standardised concept of skills, competencies and roles specialised for verification and validation;
- Team building for the specific roles and the tasks to be executed;
- Right quality of domain-specific libraries as well as right quality of cross-domain libraries;
- Interfaces between different quality engineering processes;
- Interfaces between quality engineering and release and change management;
- Interfaces between quality engineering and development processes.

In Sect. 5.1 we started a practical example from the insurance field to discuss the various dimensions and their impact on quality engineering and the respective artefacts, the quality-ware. Specialisation now delivers the picture shown in Fig. 5.12. Note: we are not discussing other industrialisation dimensions here.

From standardisation (cf. Fig. 5.9) we know the inner two circles that comprise kernel functionality and functionality for claims, contracts and persons management and the outermost circle of business units. We have now added an intermediate layer for segments of insurance business to indicate that specialists are involved who are of great benefit during development and maintenance of the insurance software but also in quality engineering. This again could also be the result of acquiring other companies.

Suppose that the V&V assets again consist of, for example, test models, test cases, test data, manual test scripts but also test results and reports. In specialisation, it is the goal not only to define specialised sub-processes for quality engineering but

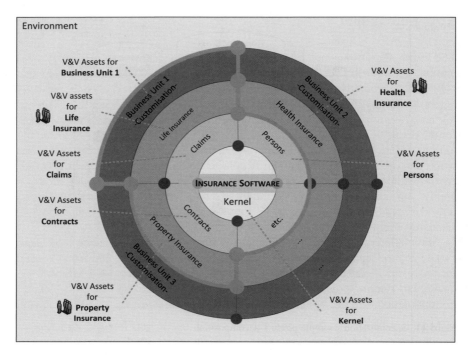

Fig. 5.12 Specialisation—insurance example

also to have the most efficient hybrid approach for assignment of specialists to those sub-processes. This is also true for the work on V&V assets and can be gained for example through specialisation due to business demands like property insurance, life insurance or car insurance. It can also be achieved by specialising along the quality engineering processes. For example, new roles like test order manager, test architect and test designer come into existence. This makes verification more efficient and cost-effective.

Quality-ware is most often moulded to the structure of the given product or parts of it. Assume that we have libraries for the kernel, for claims management, for contract management, and for persons management. Maybe there are also libraries for property insurance, life insurance or car insurance. So we can differentiate for example between:

- V&V assets for kernel to verify modules, components and specific libraries;
- V&V assets for claims management, contract management, persons management, etc., to verify functional and non-functional quality requirements;
- V&V assets for life insurance and property insurance to verify functional and non-functional quality requirements;
- V&V assets for Insurance Software of business units to verify business process quality requirements and non-functional quality requirements like performance and security within the given business unit and its customisation.

5.5 Automation

The fourth step in our method of industrialisation of quality engineering is automation. Prerequisites for automation are modularisation, standardisation and specialisation. Generally speaking, the starting point for specialisation is typically determined through the standardised, decomposed workflows, including responsibilities given to persons in a hybrid approach. This means that they are best suited for the respective role and that they are specialists in their field. This works well as long as we are willing to accept that every person is needed in the standardised workflows and cannot be efficiently replaced by automaton of repetitive tasks. Again, we totally rely on the person's capability, experience, foresight and availability but also on their speed and behaviour which could be error-prone (cf. Fig. 5.13). This is similar to the initial situation in specialisation and standardisation.

Automation always means replacing manual activities by automated ones. People are replaced by automata (robots). This definition can be applied in general for processes in car production but also for business processes, development and quality engineering processes and operations.

Automation benefits from other industrialisation dimensions:

- Modularisation goes one step further, as it opens the internal structure of automation. Automation is most efficient if functions, modules and components can be reused. Maintenance effort and complexity with subsequent unexpected side effects are reduced, giving stability and time-to-market solutions. In fact modularisation requires layered automation architectures that allow for implementation of reusable frameworks. Components relevant for the processes can be separated from components containing enriched functions for different tools used in automation. Consequently, this approach supports sustainable reuse of V&V assets for different enterprises and projects;
- Standardisation reduces the number of processes that create the same output from the same input. If processes are not standardised and variants are allowed, different automation solutions are needed. Consequently, implementation and maintenance of automation leads to high costs because of redundancy and complexity of the automation solutions;
- Specialisation separates the knowledge for different roles in the automation process. In addition to process knowledge we have technical knowledge about automation technologies and frameworks. Specialisation covers two aspects: areas with no overlap are separated and roles are defined to be covered by subject matter experts, e.g. in a factory approach. So automation makes processes more efficient but also provides a good foundation for different delivery models, like off-shore testing.

In general, when processes are analysed and considered an asset for business, one can start identifying the repetitive parts of the work for optimisation. These parts should ideally be automated. After initial implementation automation needs a

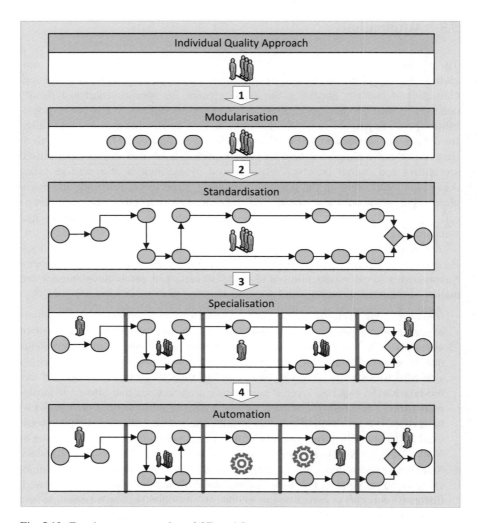

Fig. 5.13 Fourth step—automation of QE workflow

number of executions to achieve the right RoI. Therefore, for each activity within a process or even for a complete process, the possible level of automation has to be determined. There will be activities that require a lot of human interaction and run in complex environments, or a back-office application that runs in batch every night without any human interaction. Automation can expand from individual activities to the automated execution of entire process chains. A typical anti-pattern for legacy systems at this stage can be manual copy-and-paste activities from one tool into another tool, or repetitive, time-consuming quality checks on application data executed for the purpose of producing information which is already available from other systems.

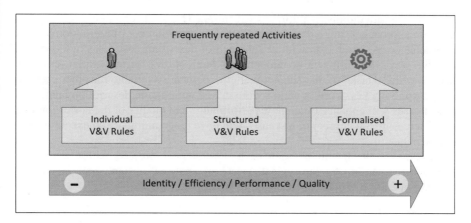

Fig. 5.14   Automation—verification and validation rules

Frequently executed activities as depicted in Fig. 5.14 are candidates for automation. They have different characteristics in terms of how they are automated.

- *Individual V&V rules:* These activities strongly depend on the individuals executing the activities. Subject matter experts execute poorly documented activities. The results depend on individual knowledge and expectations. Each repetition will differ slightly due to decisions made directly during execution. The absence of experts entails the risk of a standstill, with no alternative for replacement of experts;
- *Structured V&V rules:* The next step is to clearly address the depth of documentation. Having detailed stepwise instructions in place allows for replacement of experts by executors with different skills. This is more cost-effective and offers the opportunity for outsourcing to external specialists. Additionally, each repetition will be identical and independent of individuals. Performance can be enhanced by involving more executors, thus lowering execution time;
- *Formal V&V rules:* Structured activities are formalised in a way that allows automata (robots) to understand instructions. Formal descriptions of activities are prerequisites for generation methods, which is the most efficient way of automation.

The way from an individual, V&V-rules-approach through a structured approach to a formalised approach is itself the process of automation. For example, if there are millions of lines of code to be reviewed against the product quality characteristics of maintainability, security and licence compliance, the only way to do this efficiently is by automation. The step to a structured approach gives feasibility by sharing the work between different people. Tool-supported code reviews facilitate the implementation of appropriate technology and save time and costs. Additionally, repeatability assures the capability of benchmarking. Indicators and metrics can simply be tools to enhance application quality. Automation is essential for sustainable code quality management with respect to product quality.

A similar situation is found in test execution. The need for automation is given by agile approaches, upgrade cycles or by a sufficient number of regression tests in maintenance. Again, the structured approach of describing test cases in a comprehensive way with sufficient documentation depth allows for non-expert testers to take over these tasks so that subject matter experts are available for other creative work. Applying key-word or action-word driven automation description languages to test cases will enhance efficiency, performance and quality of the corresponding test. Increasing the number of test cases will have no great impact on execution and maintenance time.

Automation itself can be seen as a development project, within a product lifecycle, containing all the typical phases of analysis, design, implementation, test and operation. Three aspects need to be worked out:

1. Processes need to be analysed with respect to stability and repeatability. If these criteria are not fulfilled, automation addresses a moving target and as a consequence the maintenance effort is high; in the worst case, automation is not feasible at all;
2. Automation is most efficient if the design and implementation is based on generation approaches—instead of interpretation approaches—putting together the different modules to create a solution and generating the scripts for execution;
3. Automation is a long-term approach, especially when used in factories. Consequently, team organisation has to be set up in a way that maintenance and operation of the automated system can be assured. We also need quality and performance indicators for continuous measurement and control and as a foundation for continuous improvements due to better technology or process changes.

In our view, automation is regarded as a separate process with its own products. The products and solutions must be able to address different infrastructures and environments as well as a variety of quality engineering processes. Thus automation must be part of a suitable release and change management.

Looking at the details of quality engineering processes, another classification may be useful. Manual activities as part of the processes deliver a roadmap for implementing automation. This ranges from "no automation" to "automation of process execution" as depicted in Fig. 5.15. This model of automation degrees allows us to stop implementing automation when the desired degree has been achieved. Where to stop mostly depends on budget and time parameters, on skills of people and on the remaining lifecycle of the corresponding product.

Typically, the provisioning and initialisation of V&V environments (1) is a low-efficiency task set but essential for productivity of quality engineering and repeatability for regression and benchmarking. In many cases automation of this type of activities reveals many benefits. The evaluation of results after execution (2) is time-consuming and error-prone because a huge amount of data has to be analysed. Automation of evaluation allows for timely evaluation but also the analysis of the complete data set. There is no longer any need for a random sample

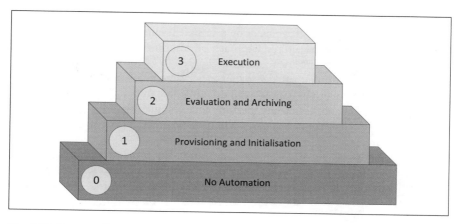

Fig. 5.15 Degrees of automation

of such data. Archiving this data automatically also means that required data can be restored during provision and initialisation. Combining all V&V activities for provisioning and initialisation, for execution and for evaluation and archiving, we reach the top degree (3). An important prerequisite for degree 3 is a stable products and V&V environment.

In Sect. 5.1 we started a practical example from the insurance field to discuss the various dimensions and their impact on quality engineering and the respective artefacts, the quality-ware. Automation now delivers the picture shown in Fig. 5.16. Note: we are not discussing other industrialisation dimensions here.

From specialisation (cf. Fig. 5.12) we know the inner three circles that comprise kernel functionality and functionality for claims, contracts and persons management and the separated skill sets for, e.g. property insurance and life insurance. We have now changed the outermost layer for segments of insurance from business units to business units per country, just to indicate that the more we can use standardised quality assets, the more we can benefit when applying them to many organisational units. This again could be the result of acquiring other national or international companies.

Suppose that the V&V assets again consist of, for example, test models, test cases, test data, manual test scripts but also test results and reports. In automation it is the goal to have automated V&V assets for all or parts of processes. In this dimension we need specialists for the implementation as well as appropriate tools and frameworks. For example, new roles like test automation architects, test automation administrator and test automation engineers come into existence. This makes verification more efficient and cost-effective.

Quality-ware is most often moulded to the structure of the given product or parts of it. Let us assume that we have libraries for the kernel, for claims management, for contract management, and for persons management. Maybe there are also libraries for property insurance, life insurance or car insurance for a business unit in one or

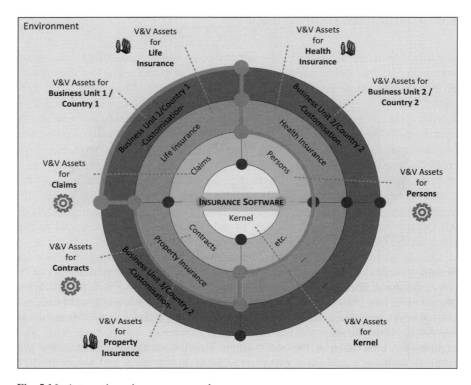

Fig. 5.16 Automation—insurance example

more countries. But we have also the V&V automation assets as indicated above. So we can differentiate for example between:

- V&V assets for kernel to verify modules, components and specific libraries either manually or automated;
- V&V assets for claims management, contract management, persons management, etc., to verify functional and non-functional quality requirements either manually or automated;
- V&V assets for life insurance and property insurance to verify functional and non-functional quality requirements either manually or automated;
- V&V assets for Insurance Software of business units to verify business process quality requirements and non-functional quality requirements like performance and security within the given business unit and its customisation; here too we have the choice between manual or automated procedures;
- Implementation and maintenance of V&V automation assets;
- Administration of the automated V&V system.

5.6   Continuous Improvement

The fifth step in our method of industrialisation of quality engineering is continuous improvement. Continuous improvement is not a value in itself. The four dimensions of industrialisation described so far are based on dedicated company goals. Processes and products are moulded to these goals. Quality governance and quality management are disciplines to ensure that those goals are achieved and continuous improvement provides the means to regularly and systematically analyse the organisation, its processes and (work) products on the way to productive and cost-effective ICT.

Prerequisites, as is the case for standardisation, specialisation and automation, are therefore not needed. Generally speaking, the starting point for continuous improvement can be all the situations described above, beginning with the Individual Quality Approach, going through all industrialisation dimensions and finally reaching the Quality Services Factory (cf. Fig. 5.17).

Quality governance and quality management are organisational anchors for defining quality goals and establishing and controlling quality activities with respect to the defined goals. Continuous improvement is the mechanism of continuously observing the quality management and quality governance system to adapt both systems to a changing world based on the experiences gathered from information on how the components in the system interact and behave. This also includes the adaptation of the goal system. Continuous improvement is the key factor in defining and implementing the right quality. It gives us trustworthy ICT processes and ICT products, not oversized but also not hard to achieve. It provides the mechanisms for evolving industrialisation from effectiveness to efficiency by refining modularisation, standardisation, specialisation and automation, as controlled by the frame created by quality governance, quality management and portfolio management.

Even if we have well-structured tasks (modularisation), standardised processes, methods and procedures (standardisation), defined skills and roles, trained people, defined recruitment and qualification programmes (specialisation) and, last but not least, established automation frameworks (automation)—continuous reflection on the enterprise's situation that takes into account changing markets, changing business conditions, new business models, current capacities and capabilities of the enterprise is required. To decide thoroughly on enterprise changes we also need key performance indicators and key quality indicators for ICT processes and ICT products. For continuous improvement to be applied effectively, it needs to be initialised with the first steps of industrialisation.

All aspects described upfront on our journey of industrialisation of quality engineering should be checked after implementation. Feedback and experiences need to be collected and provided in a Quality Intelligence portal for sustainable decisions. In the first stages, personal feedback and impressions are the most valuable; as we add more details and measurable concepts for quality this will be

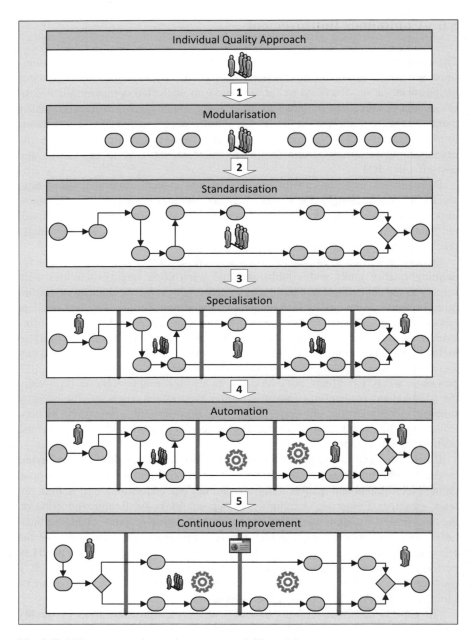

Fig. 5.17 Fifth step—continuous improvement of QE workflow

increasingly based on facts and a quantitative understanding of the processes and results. An important link to the management disciplines is:

- Portfolio management defines the goals and investments;
- Quality management defines the rules; and
- Quality governance defines the controls.

A structured approach for continuous improvement provides mechanisms and responsibilities to link the improvement ideas to the named management areas. This ensures alignment between initiatives and improvements; it helps to understand business needs and reflects on the balance between investments and risks.

Test automation, for example, is given a certain time for maintenance and execution before an ICT product is deployed. Test automation fulfils the goal of getting high regression coverage with a short duration in execution time. A highly flexible test automation framework can compensate late delivery of changed applications by shortening the time for maintenance. This requires additional effort and people to create a highly flexible framework and to cover the maintenance work.

Once continuous improvement is in place, different and new questions will arise. Why is delivery so late? Why do we have such a high number of changes? Are they based on requirements or on defects found very late in the development process? The organisation can then scrutinise its decision: should we invest in test automation or should we instead invest in process optimisation on delivery or earlier testing. This would perhaps lead to new or modified tasks.

Depending on company size, degree of interaction with partners, and product composition the need for establishing levels of industrialisation has to be determined and introduced in a scalable manner. Many benefits from earlier industrialisation steps can already be leveraged at lower levels. In addition, each of these steps can be implemented in parts of the organisation, i.e. industrialisation can be in place for the specific V&V stages like system testing without being applied to user acceptance testing.

In Sect. 5.1 we started a practical example from the insurance field to discuss the various dimensions and their impact on quality engineering and the respective artefacts, the quality-ware. Continuous improvement can now be applied when enterprises start considering cloud technology and deciding on its use. The last picture of our running example from the insurance field is given in Fig. 5.18.

Concluding this section on continuous improvement, we can ask some questions in our example which have to be answered in a concrete situation:

- What has to be changed in enterprise processes products?
- Which V&V assets are affected by those changes?
- Is quality engineering as a whole a candidate for change?
- Can we make use of cloud technology for the quality engineering task?
- Can we apply the current V&V assets to cloud technology?
- What is different when V&V assets are not cloud compatible and a decision is taken not to apply this?

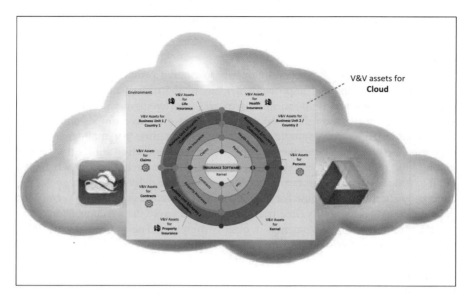

Fig. 5.18   Insurance example—continuous improvement

5.7   The Resulting House of Quality

The final picture of the industrialisation process has been developed from Sect. 5.1 up to 5.7. At the end of our journey that started with an Individual Quality Approach and took us through the various dimension of industrialisation—modularisation, standardisation, specialisation, automation, continuous improvement—we reach the Quality Services Factory. Remember the starting point and now look at the final situation in Fig. 5.19.

Within the second box we now find a decomposed workflow consisting of four phases, with the initial phase on the left, the completion phase on the right and in parallel two assembly lines for the execution of equal tasks. Specially qualified people as well as suitable automation frameworks are operating and running in these two flows for efficient execution of incoming orders. For a detailed description we refer to Chap. 6.

The resulting "Industrialised House of Quality" now contains all the industrialisation dimensions starting from IQA and ending with QSF and, additionally, is established and enabled by the management disciplines of Quality Governance and Quality Management (cf. Fig. 5.20).

Quality Governance and Quality Management, finally, complete the industrialisation approach to build a House of Quality that drives the stepwise evolvement of the five dimensions. Similar to assessment and process models like SPICE (ISO-15504 2011) and CMMI (Chrissis et al. 2011), a level concept is integrated in our House of Quality that reflects the sequence of adequate steps towards an industrialised approach to quality engineering. Being on a specific point between

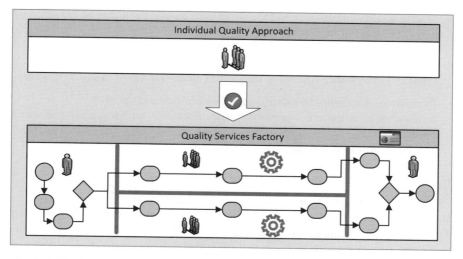

Fig. 5.19   The industrialisation process is completed—QSF

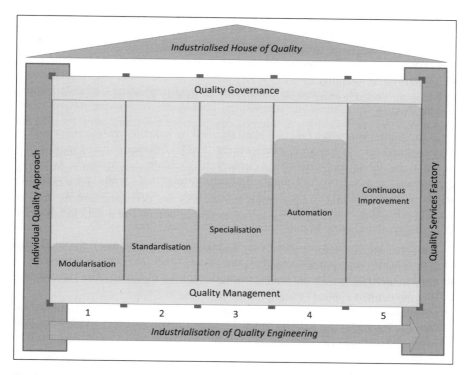

Fig. 5.20   Industrialised House of Quality

one end of quality engineering and the target configuration can then be indicated by a degree, i.e. level of industrialisation.

As mentioned above, Quality Governance and Quality Management are essential disciplines to successfully apply industrialisation.

Quality Governance following the COBIT definition (ISACA 2012) ensures:

• Evaluation of stakeholder quality needs, conditions and options;
• Evaluation of balance between enterprise objectives set for quality goals and business needs;
• Setting of priorities for implementation;
• Monitoring of compliance with governance related KQIs and KPIs;
• Decision-making based on monitoring results.

In most enterprises, Quality Governance is not a separate discipline. If visible at all, it is not recognised as an important part of defining quality direction and evolvement of the organisation. We suggest making it part of the overall governance and associating responsibility to the board of directors under the leadership of the chairperson. Specific quality governance responsibilities may be delegated to special organisational structures at an appropriate level, particularly in larger, complex enterprises.

Quality Management following the COBIT definition (ISACA 2012) ensures:

• Definition of a system of activities and measures mapped to quality objectives set by Quality Governance;
• Planning of activities to achieve the quality objectives;
• Establishment of activities to achieve the quality objectives;
• Monitoring of compliance to KQI and KPI;
• Mapping and reporting of achievements to quality objectives set by Quality Governance.

In most enterprises this function is established by a quality management role as representative of the top-level management (CxO). Besides defining goals, it is essential to define and establish a system to evaluate and improve company performance and ICT product quality. Indicators and metrics with right granularity are required to break down the goals and objectives to objects, characteristics and checkpoints. This is depicted in Fig. 5.21 and bridges the gap between Quality Governance and Quality Management (cf. Simon and Simon 2010).

• **Objects**: which artefacts should be monitored and controlled? Examples are architecture, code, processes and resources;
• **Characteristics**: which properties will be important for monitoring and controlling the defined context? Examples are provided in Chap. 3;
• **Checkpoints**: which objects should have which characteristics, or a combination thereof? Examples are given in Table 3.7 where characteristics are associated for every artefact type or artefact;
• **Indicators**: what are the threshold values and weights at various checkpoints that show anomalies and problems? Examples are earned value, code coverage and test coverage;

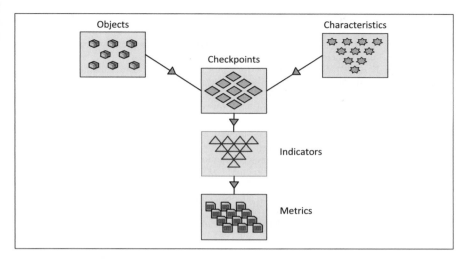

Fig. 5.21 The Y-Model for quality control

- **Metrics**: how are the indicators measured? Examples are budget, current costs, risk level, number of requirements and system volume.

To implement this approach, first select the corresponding objects and determine the relevant characteristics. Then relate the objects with the corresponding characteristics. Define which values indicate an upcoming risk and last but not least, define metrics such that the indicators can be measured. All objects, characteristics and indicators can also be weighted if necessary.

For example, suppose a company has decided at the strategic layer to increase profitability by implementing the industrialisation dimensions. To achieve this, test automation as the object needs to become more efficient; this is the characteristic. The checkpoint will be "check test automation for efficiency". Examples of indicators are "too many staff per test case" and "too small a degree of automation". Number of staff, number of automated test cases, and total number of test cases are metrics to calculate such indicators. By applying weights and thresholds at the indicator level, transparency is achieved and decisions can be taken.

References and Links

Avaloq (2013) Industrialisierung, Erreichen Sie Kostensenkungen mittels Industrialisierung. http://www.avaloq.com/de/bpo/industrialisierung/. Retrieved 18 Nov 2013
BITKOM (2010) Industrielle Softwareentwicklung, Leitfaden und Orientierungshilfe. BITKOM, Berlin
Buxmann P, Diefenbach H, Hess T (2008) Die Softwareindustrie: Ökonomische Prinzipien, Strategien, Perspektiven. Springer, Berlin

Capgemini (2012) Studie IT-Trends 2012—Business-IT-Alignment sichert die Zukunft. Capgemini, Berlin

Chrissis M, Konrad M, Shrum S (2011) CMMI for development: guidelines for process integration and product improvement, 3rd edn. Pearson Education, Boston

Free D, Wang E (2013) Magic quadrant for international retail core banking. Gartner ID: G00252184. http://www.gartner.com/technology/reprints.do?id=1-1LRK80J&ct=131015& st=sb#. Posted 8 Oct 2013. Retrieved 13 Dec 2013

ISACA (2012) COBIT 5—a business framework for the governance and management of enterprise IT. ISACA

ISO-15504 (2011) Information technology—process assessment. International Organisation for Standardisation (ISO), Geneva

ITIL (2011) ITIL lifecycle publication suite. The Stationary Office, Norwich

Koomen T, van der Alst L, Broekman B, Vroon M (2008) TMap Next—Ein praktischer Leitfaden für ergebnisorientes Softwaretesten. dpunkt, Heidelberg

Schekkerman J (2006) How to survive in the jungle of enterprise architecture frameworks: creating or choosing an enterprise architecture framework. Trafford Publishing, Bloomington, IN

Simon F, Simon D (2010) Qualitäts-Risiko-Management—Ganzheitliche IT Projektsteuerung. Logos, Berlin

Spillner A, Roßner T, Winter M, Linz T (2011) Praxiswissen Softwaretest—Testmanagement: Aus- und Weiterbildung zum Certified Tester—advanced Level nach ISTQB-Standard. dpunkt, Heidelberg

TestSPICE SIG (2012) The TestSPICE PAM—Process Assessment Model. http://www.intacs. info/index.php/testspice. Retrieved on 16 Dec 2013

TestSPICE SIG (2012) The TestSPICE PRM—Process Reference Model. http://www.intacs.info/ index.php/testspice. Retrieved on 16 Dec 2013

UML (2011) OMG Unified Modeling Language (OMG UML). Version 2.4.1. http://www.omg. org/spec/UML/2.4.1/. Retrieved on 16 Dec 2013

van Veenendaal E, Wells B (2012) Test Maturity Model integration (TMMi)—guidelines for test process improvement. UTN Publishers, Den Bosch

Wiki-Industrialisation (2013). http://simple.wikipedia.org/wiki/Industrialisation. Retrieved 13 Dec 2013

Wiki-Industrie (2013) http://de.wikipedia.org/wiki/Industrie. Retrieved 13 Dec 2013

WSDL (2007) Web Services Description Language (WSDL) Version 2.0. http://www.w3.org/TR/ #tr_WSDL. Retrieved on 16 Dec 2013

Young A, et al (2008) Gartner on outsourcing, 2008–2009. http://www.gartner.com/id=844219. Retrieved 13 Nov 2013

 http://media2.giga.de/2012/05/cloud1.jpg. Retrieved 15 Dec 2013

Chapter 6
The Quality Services Factory

An increasing number of companies across various industries have implemented an internal shared-services model that delivers ICT services to their end users. The objective of the shared-services team is to drive enhancements and improvements of the existing business applications and operating systems. In addition, they focus on the consolidation and replacement of legacy systems that are the result of acquisitions or have been accumulated over time as part of the overall operating system.

As previously discussed in Chaps. 3–5 we are convinced that a holistic approach, focused on quality, which combines product orientation with industrialised quality engineering and a sound notion of right quality will reduce costs. The ultimate goal of industrialisation as discussed in Chap. 5 is the so-called Quality Services Factory. It is helpful to align with a strategic partner to define, build and operate such a model. There are several reasons to involve a specialist, specifically acceleration of model implementation, experience, best practices, independence and flexibility. The receiving organisation can bring knowledge and experiences in their own domain and methodologies. The specialist organisation can bring many years of experiences in implementing and improving the necessary processes across a wide array of customers.

Transforming a current quality organisation into a Quality Services Factory requires various aspects and tasks to be considered upfront. This is independent of whether the QSF is operated completely internally or operated internally or in collaboration with a strategic partner. These various aspects and tasks comprise analysis of the current situation and definition of the QSF concept containing the services, the internal processes and structures, the external processes and escalation mechanisms and the cooperation model with business and other ICT organisations in the company. This will be discussed in the subsequent sections.

M. Wieczorek et al., *Systems and Software Quality*,
DOI 10.1007/978-3-642-39971-8_6, © Springer-Verlag Berlin Heidelberg 2014

6.1   Our Factory Approach

Remember from previous chapters of this book that our industrialisation model consists of the following integral disciplines and dimensions to bring an enterprise to a cost-effective Quality Services Factory:

1. Industrialisation dimensions

   (a) Modularisation—equal or similar tasks can make use of existing quality assets such as quality models and associated verification and validation assets;
   (b) Standardisation—best practice templates and processes can be used for every maintenance and product development project;
   (c) Specialisation—people who work in such a services factory can use their knowledge and experience from previous tasks in the same or a similar domain;
   (d) Automation—standardised processes or process parts can be conducted using existing automation frameworks and scripts;
   (e) Continuous improvement—the feedback control loop to promote improvements of the other four dimensions and of the QSF as a whole.

2. Management disciplines

   (a) Quality Governance—ensuring that right quality of the respective artefacts and V&V assets is transparent and making transparent the risks of particular ICT products when applied in production;
   (b) Quality Management—planning, building, running and monitoring all activities in alignment with the direction set by the governance body to achieve the enterprise objectives, including measurement of quality and performance characteristics.

All services offered by a Quality Services Factory in steady state are based on quality assets that are already available and evolving. If assets are not available it will be necessary to first define them and then go into a steady-state phase of the QSF. In our systemic view, a Quality Services Factory is a black box (cf. Fig. 6.1) transforming specific input into output that has been defined in the corresponding service catalogue.

In our case, the input to the QSF consists of a so-called "Quality Service Request" to initiate the factory's processing. Additional material has to be supplied to the factory along with this request. Most often the material is contained in databases as part of particular software tools. "Supply" here means either to provide access to that tool for the people of the QSF or to provide it as electronic data files or as paper documentation. At least the following **input** must be provided:

- Requirements—what has to be implemented;
- Quality model—what has to be proven;
- Business process portfolio—what has changed in business;
- ICT landscape—what has changed in ICT.

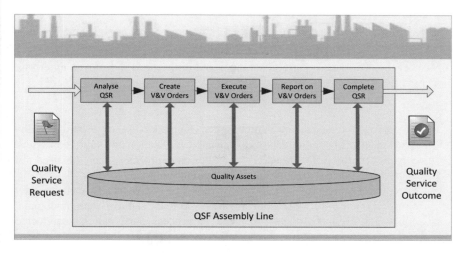

Fig. 6.1 Quality Services Factory

The list of all input artefacts depends on the particular service and forms part of the corresponding Service Level Agreement.

Likewise, the output of the QSF is given as a so-called "Quality Service Outcome" to the requesting unit, which has to accept the final QSO. Here, too, additional material has to be supplied to the requesting unit. As above, this QSO material is contained in databases as part of particular software tools or it will be provided as electronic data files or as paper documentation. At least the following **output** must be provided:

- Quality report—what are the service results and the remaining quality/risk level;
- Lessons learned—what has been learned during execution.

The list of all output artefacts depends on the particular service and forms part of the corresponding SLA.

A practical implementation of the QSF based on these principles is, for example, the "SQS Test Automation FaQtory" as briefly described in Kasmalkar (2012).

Factory Processing

The Quality Services Factory provides a number of services that will be delivered following a Quality Service Request as indicated above. Such a request is initiated from the corresponding site defined in the factory contract. The request will then be executed following the process on the right (cf. Fig. 6.2).

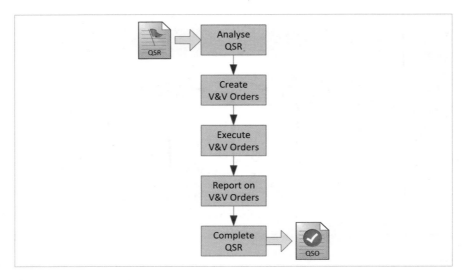

Fig. 6.2 Factory processing

The first sub-process is the analysis of the QSR. The request, including the associated input, will be analysed with respect to conformance to the contract and to completeness, consistency and tangibility of the associated input. After evaluation of the request it is either rejected or accepted. It is rejected if, for example, the content is incomplete, inconsistent, or incomprehensible or the actual frame conditions of the Quality Services Factory do not allow for performing the request. If it is accepted the next sub-process will be started, where so-called Verification and Validation orders are generated and handed over for execution. This is given in the next sub-process. Each V&V order contains exactly one QSF service. The service is rendered following the predefined process description and delivers the corresponding result. During execution the process is monitored and controlled by an internal quality manager and continuous reporting is provided about the progress made by the assembly line involved. Once the final result has been produced the process is completed and the outcome is collected for delivery to the requesting unit.

As in the assembly line of manufacturing, we use the term "Order Execution Line" or "QSF assembly line" for the corresponding factory selected for executing a particular order. The OXL will be located somewhere in the world as part of a sourcing centre where suitable know-how is present and the execution schedule allows for time conditions to be met. Besides know-how and time, the decision for a particular order execution line depends on a few additional parameters:

- V&V order maturity, i.e. the maturity of the given material as part of the V&V order;
- Data protection level, i.e. the degree to which the data involved during V&V order execution has to meet the data protection rules of the corresponding company;

Table 6.1 Example for selecting the suitable OXL

V&V Order	V&V Order Maturity	Privacy Protection Level		Delivery / Order Execution Line
	low	low	→	onsite
	medium	low	→	onsite or nearshore or offshore
	high	low	→	onsite or nearshore or offshore
	low	high	→	onsite
	medium	high	→	onsite or nearshore
	high	high	→	onsite or nearshore

- Location, i.e. the country where the company is located;
- Language, i.e. the language used at the company site.

To get more insight into these rules let us look at the example depicted in Table 6.1. Different parameter values are possible and are defined as follows:

- V&V order maturity

  - Low—face-to-face client involvement needed;
  - Medium—not highly standardised, but client involvement is not needed;
  - High—highly standardized.

- Privacy protection level

  - Low—personal data is not used or data is anonymised;
  - High—personal data is used.

- Delivery/Order execution line

  - Onsite—QSF at the company's premises;
  - Nearshore—QSF at the premises of an outsourcing partner but in the same country;
  - Offshore—QSF at the premises of an outsourcing partner but in another country.

The OXL will be dependent on the language of the respective project and the language of the delivery centre. For example, if the company is British and the project language is English, the delivery centre could be in Northern Ireland. If the company is German and the project language is English, a nearshore centre could be chosen if English is available in the nearshore centre; if not, an English-speaking offshore centre must be selected. If the company is German and the project language is also German, one option is nearshore delivery; another option could be offshore if and only if that centre has German language available.

Quality Assets

As previously discussed, there are various quality assets that can be defined, maintained and applied during the lifecycle of an enterprise's ICT landscape.

Some of these are owned by the QSF whereas others are owned by other business or ICT units of the enterprise. In this factory approach, different quality assets are assigned to the corresponding release of the business process portfolio and to every ICT system of the ICT system landscape. Quality assets usually comprise different types of real and virtual artefacts. In this chapter, the following categories are relevant:

- Documentation like specifications, concepts and templates; examples are quality gate concept, test concept, test staging concept, test automation concept, test reports including metrics, test plan and test data management concepts;
- Methodology such as methods and procedures for test modelling, test case design, test execution, measurement and reporting;
- Software tools like test management tools, performance tools, code coverage tools, and dashboards;
- Quality-ware like validation rules, verification rules, test models, test case portfolio, test data, test scripts and test environments, including test databases;
- Knowledge and experience of the QSF employees, such as business domain know-how, validation and verification know-how, test know-how, and tool know-how.

It is mandatory to have a sound release and configuration management in place because there are artefacts owned by people outside the QSF and other artefacts that are owned by the QSF itself. At every point in time, we need to know which version of the artefacts and quality assets is valid and can be applied for the validation and verification of quality criteria. Let us review a factory processing example where the QSR contains a manual functional test to be performed by the QSF due to a change request (cf. Fig. 6.3).

The input here comprises:

- QSR—Manual Functional Test due to a change request (CR);
- Documentation of business processes BP_1 and BP_4, which are relevant for system SYS_1;
- Documentation of the ICT system SYS_1, including its channels CH_1 and CH_2;
- Documentation of the change request; and
- Documentation of the product quality model.

The output here consists of:

- The QSO—Request for Acceptance;
- The test Report; and
- The lessons learned.

The factory owned quality assets in this case are:

- Quality-ware containing

  - New test cases for system SYS_1 due to the change request;
  - Test case portfolio for system SYS_1—release Rel X;
  - Test case portfolio for system SYS_1—release Rel X + 1;

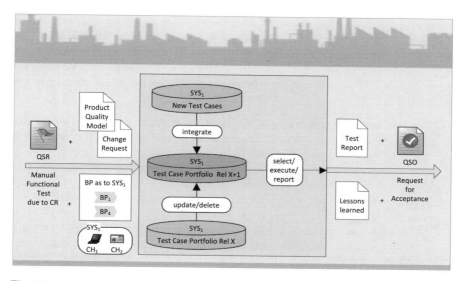

Fig. 6.3 Manual functional test due to CR

- Documentation of the test results after execution.

There may be more quality assets or assets belonging to the quality-ware that have to be changed, such as test scripts or databases, but we have assumed here that no further changes are necessary.

The example above was chosen from the operational layer of an enterprise and its daily business. The next example is from the tactical layer (cf. Fig. 6.4). Here, we assume that all quality assets are objects for change. Which parts are really affected must become clear from the business process optimisation documentation and the quality models at this layer (cf. Chap. 3). A QSR is initiated by strategic or tactical changes in the enterprise, e.g. changes in the business process architecture due to efficiency improvements.

The input here comprises:

- QSR—Test Asset Optimisation due to business process optimisation;
- Documentation of the business process portfolio;
- Documentation of the business process optimisation; and
- Documentation of the strategic quality/risk model.

The output here consists of:

- The QSO—Request for Acceptance;
- The optimisation results; and
- The lessons learned.

The factory owned quality assets in this case are:

- Quality-ware containing

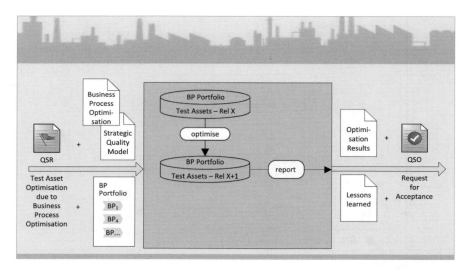

Fig. 6.4   Test Asset Optimisation due to business process optimisation

- Test assets for the business process portfolio – release Rel X;
- Test assets for the business process portfolio – release Rel X + 1;
- Documentation of the optimisation results.

The last example shows that a project does not have to be the driver of changes to the quality assets but that it is part of the lifecycle of the end product and decisions at the tactical layer.

QSF Services

At the beginning of this chapter we discussed that a QSF is set up by the internal shared-services provider. Goals are defined for quality engineering to achieve increased effectiveness and efficiency and, therefore, reduced costs in this field of ICT.

The services of a Quality Services Factory are distinguished by the following three categories which we will call **service cluster**:

- Core services (Core, possibly subdivided);
- Management services (Management); and
- Supporting services (Supporting).

Core services (COR) are those for which the factory is built and for which the factory approach can be applied in a strict sense. For example, proving the code quality of a software application can be assigned to a QSF as well as business

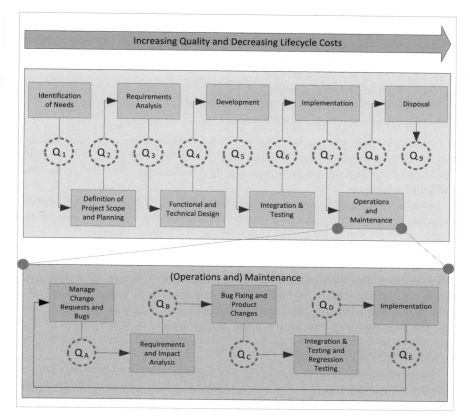

Fig. 6.5 Quality lifecycle equals the product lifecycle

process-based testing after maintenance of the corresponding software. A further example is the optimisation of a test case portfolio for some systems in the ICT systems landscape.

Management services (MAN) are necessary for planning, monitoring and control of all quality service requests and subsequently V&V orders. Services from this service cluster cannot be executed alone, as they always accompany core and supporting services. Examples are on-/off-boarding of resources, V&V order management and defect management.

Supporting services (SUP) are those that enable the core services to be executed in a particular environment. For example, if tools support the validation and verification of artefacts, such tools have to be set up, maintained and operated maybe as part of a company's private cloud.

What are appropriate candidates for outsourcing in a QSF? From Chap. 2 we know that activities and tasks for which the five dimensions of our industrialisation model can be applied to a great extent are suitable candidates. To find answers, let us look at our model of a quality lifecycle (cf. Fig. 6.5).

Between quality gates Q_2 and Q_7 there are some verification and/or validation tasks that allow for a partial or complete sourcing to a QSF, i.e.:

- Validation and verification of requirements;
- Verification of functional design;
- Verification of technical design;
- Validation and verification of quality-ware; and
- Verification of software and systems.

Obviously, there are similar tasks in the box "(Operations and) Maintenance" that we do not consider here. What is part of sourcing and what remains in the traditional mode depends on the results of a "QSF readiness check" during the setup and transition phase.

Let us examine a QSF service configuration (cf. Table 6.2) that might be suitable for verifying a legacy system with change requests during operations and maintenance (cf. also Chap. 3 for quality characteristics of legacy systems).

To be able to easily distinguish the services in a Quality Service Request or V&V order it is useful to associate each service with a so-called "service identification number" that is unique in the QSF service portfolio. An option field indicates whether a certain service is "mandatory", "optional" or "recommended". If a service is offered by the QSF but not yet applicable, this is indicated by "no". The option value may not be the same for all quality services factories. This depends on the strategic setup of the QSF and its complete and consistent functioning during the lifecycle.

A service definition then drills down to the characteristics of each service. Our systemic view allows us to define a service as a black box. Besides the characteristics already mentioned (SID, service cluster, service name and an option), the following details have to be provided:

- Service description;
- Additional conditions;
- Roles;
- Service input;
- Service result;
- Service Level Agreement; and
- Invoicing.

Table 6.3 shows an example of a service called "Re-test of defects" as part of our proposed service portfolio above.

Roles and Responsibilities

Operating a Quality Services Factory and taking responsibility for the various results requires different roles with corresponding responsibilities. Some of these

Table 6.2 A sample QSF service configuration for legacy systems

SID	Service Cluster	Service Name	Option
QSF-COR -S01	Core	Requirements Analysis with Quality Feedback along the Quality Model ReqQMod	optional
QSF-COR -S02	Core	Functional Design Analysis with Quality Feedback along the Quality Model DocQMod	optional
QSF-COR -S03	Core	Architecture Analysis with Quality Feedback along the Quality Model ArchQMod	optional
QSF-COR -S04	Core	Code Analysis with Quality Feedback along the Quality Model CodeQMod and DataQMod	recommended
QSF-COR -S05	Core	Generation of Quality-Ware with Quality Feedback along the defined Quality Models	no
QSF-COR -S06	Core	Maintenance of Quality-Ware	mandatory
QSF-COR -S07	Core	Quality Asset Optimisation	optional
QSF-COR -S08	Core	Product Testing	mandatory
QSF-COR -S09	Core	Business Process Testing	mandatory
QSF-COR -S10	Core	Functional Testing	mandatory
QSF-COR -S11	Core	Explorative Testing	no
QSF-COR -S12	Core	Load/Performance Testing	no
QSF-COR -S13	Core	Security Testing	no
QSF-COR -S14	Core	Re-Test of Defects along the corresponding Quality Model and Defect List	mandatory
QSF-MAN-S15	Management	Test Management	mandatory – overhead to other services –
QSF-MAN-S16	Management	Order Management	mandatory – overhead to other services –
QSF-MAN-S17	Management	Defect Management	mandatory – overhead to other services –
QSF-SUP-S18	Supporting	Test Tool Setup, Maintenance and Operation	mandatory
QSF-SUP-S19	Supporting	Infrastructure and Environment Management	mandatory
QSF-SUP-S20	Supporting	Test Data Management	mandatory

are taken by the company itself and others are taken by the internal shared-services provider or the external QSF partner.

Table 6.4 provides a brief overview of roles and their responsibilities at the company site. The roles reflect our view of roles and responsibilities as part of our holistic quality approach for an enterprise.

The roles and responsibilities within the QSF are slightly more differentiated. Besides the management roles, experts are needed who can analyse, conduct and finalise the corresponding tasks along the V&V orders. Following our proposal of a service catalogue above we have topics like ICT architecture, development and coding and testing. Therefore, our proposal for suitable roles is provided in Table 6.5.

Table 6.3 Example of a service definition

SID	Service Cluster	Service Name	Option
QSF-COR -S17	Core	Re-Test of Defects along the corresponding Quality Model and Defects List	mandatory

Service Description
- All defect tickets assigned to the QSF will be re-tested.
- If the result of the re-test of a certain ticket is negative, i.e., the defect still exists, this ticket is directly given back to development and maintenance.
- If a new defect is recognised, a new ticket will be raised regarding the valid defect classification scheme.
- If interdependencies between tickets are recognised, a link will be set between those tickets.

Additional Conditions
- The description of all associated tickets must be complete, i.e.:
  - re-test scenarios and test steps;
  - use case and database;
  - screenshot for comparison;
  - description of the expected result;
  - the version number from which the defect is fixed;
  - point in time from which the defect can be verified.
- The test data needed for the re-test must be provided anonymised by the test environment.
- The test database must be compatible with the major version of the software for which the ticket is to be verified.
- The new software (build) must be installed completely in the corresponding test infrastructure.
- Tickets that are re-tested as part of other services will not be re-tested by this service.

Roles
Test Analyst.

Service Input
All defect tickets assigned to the QSF.

Service Outcome
The results of the re-tests will be provided as part of the UAT report or the test execution report.

Service Level Agreement
- The service level is measured by KPI-TM-01.
- The time periods can be agreed on request.

Invoicing
The invoicing for this service is asset/value based. The rate card is part of the corresponding contract.

Table 6.4 Roles and responsibilities at company site

Role	Description
ICT Lead	Responsible for the Company's entire ICT Landscape.
Product Owner	Responsible for a certain ICT System within the Company's ICT Landscape.
Programme Lead	Responsible for a particular ICT Programme.
Project Lead	Responsible for a particular ICT Project.
Development Lead	Responsible for the Development of a particular Project/Programme.
Quality Lead	Responsible for all Quality Requirements and their Implementation.
QSF Manager	Responsible for the Interface to the QSF.

Table 6.5 Roles and responsibilities at QSF site

Role	Description
QSF Lead	Overall responsibility for the performance of the QSF.
QSR Manager	Responsible for quality service requests, including planning, monitoring, and control of service delivery.
Defect Manager	Responsible for all defects raised within quality service requests.
Quality Analyst	Responsible for deriving quality assets.
Tool Expert	Responsible for administration and maintenance of the tools.
Business Expert	Analysis of business requirements.
Technology Expert	Analysis of technology requirements, administration of infrastructure and testing tools.
ICT Architect	Analysis of ICT architecture.
Code Expert	Analysis of software code.
Test Analyst	Creation of test assets (e.g. logical and physical test cases).
Test Engineer	Automation of test cases.
Tester	Execution of manual and automated test cases, analysis of test results.

Resources

On- and off-boarding of resources is a critical internal QSF process. Flexibility and performance of the QSF are strongly dependent on this process. For example, more flexibility is given if the internal shared-services provider has more than one option to disseminate the workload to different sourcing centres of the factory. Whether this provider has set up those centres for itself or involves an external partner is also part of the strategic concept for the QSF. The skills of the corresponding employees are important for the performance of such factories. These skills comprise knowledge and experience with the services to be executed and, to a certain extent, domain knowledge and know-how in validation and verification of the corresponding artefacts. It is indispensable to have suitable training plans and supervision systems in place.

Infrastructure

Besides the people, there is another prerequisite for the productivity of a QSF, namely the infrastructure. This comprises buildings, e.g. workplaces and working environment, computer systems, communication infrastructure, software, database systems and tools.

All services mentioned above will be executed with the support of many different people, e.g. technical staff, caretaker, etc.

Reporting

There are two categories in reporting from QSF to the company, i.e., quality reporting and performance reporting. Whereas quality reports present the current metrics for the quality development of software solutions, the performance reports represent the actual state of the performance of selected processes and SLAs. Reports may contain tables, diagrams and text describing the situation in accordance with the goals of the report and contract. An overview of reports provided by a QSF is presented in Table 6.6.

Typical report examples are also depicted in Fig. 6.6. Reports can be provided by a tool that collects all the data during the whole lifecycle, a so-called Quality Intelligence tool, or by documents containing text, sheets and diagrams. The type of reporting is also determined in the corresponding QSF concept.

Key Quality Indicators/Key Performance Indicators

The Quality of Service that QSF provides on request is defined as a Service Level Agreement as part of the corresponding contract between the QSF provider and the company. The QoS can be defined for a particular service, for a Quality Service Request or for the QSF as a whole. In all three cases, the term Quality of Service will be used. The QoS can then be monitored and controlled by a QI portal. Sample tables and charts are depicted in Fig. 6.6.

Basic to Service Level Agreements (see below) are a set of Key Performance Indicators and a set of Key Quality Indicators. Table 6.7 provides proposals for a useful KPI as well as a useful KQI that we have applied in many cases.

Service Level Agreement

If the Quality of Service cannot be measured it is presumed that it is high following state-of-the-art methods, procedures, and tools known from the market. For all other situations, the QoS and its SLA are defined in Table 6.8.

Collaboration and Escalation

In order to make the performance of a QSF as efficient and effective as possible, governance and escalation procedures have to be defined. Governance is based on the reporting defined above. The governance model is defined for all three

Table 6.6 Quality and performance reports

RID	Name	Type	Goal	Frequency
QSF-R-01	QSR report	Performance	Transparency about the actual status of QSRs.	monthly
QSF-R-02	User Acceptance Report	Quality	Transparency about the effort, findings, and recommendations for Go-live.	for every acceptance
QSF-R-03	Test Case Generation Report	Performance	Transparency about the generation of manual and automated test cases.	monthly
QSF-R-04	Test Case Maintenance Report	Performance	Transparency about the maintenance of manual and automated test cases.	monthly
QSF-R-05	Test Case Portfolio Report	Performance	Transparency about the optimisation of the test cases portfolio.	monthly
QSF-R-06	Regression Testing Report	Quality	Transparency about the effort and findings.	monthly
QSF-R-07	Explorative Testing Report	Quality	Transparency about the effort and findings.	monthly
QSF-R-08	Test Case Execution Report	Quality	Transparency about the effort and findings, including re-tests.	monthly
QSF-R-09	Requirements Analysis Report	Quality	Transparency about the effort and findings.	monthly
QSF-R-10	Load/Performance Testing Report	Quality	Transparency about the effort and findings.	monthly
QSF-R-11	Security Testing Report	Quality	Transparency about the effort and findings.	monthly
QSF-R-12	Architecture Review Report	Quality	Transparency about the effort and findings.	monthly
QSF-R-13	Service Level Compliance Report	Performance	Transparency about the actual status of service level compliance.	quarterly
QSF-R-14	Controlling Report	Performance	Transparency about the effort and findings.	monthly
QSF-R-15	Implementation Report	Performance and Quality	Transparency about the current status of the software development.	monthly

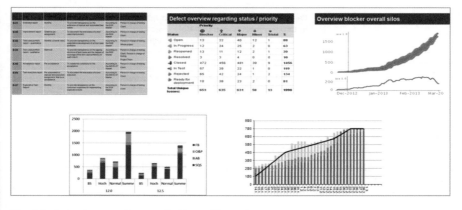

Fig. 6.6 Reporting samples provided by a QI portal

Table 6.7 KQI / KPI

KID	KQI/KPI	Description
KPI-01	Adherence to Delivery Dates	• The delivery date is the date on which the result of executing a service or V&V order is provided to the company. • It is associated to a service or a V&V order. • The standard target value is five working days from the starting point. • Individual agreements are allowed and must be stated as part of the corresponding service or V&V order.
KQI-01	Business Disruption	• Business disruption is given if and when a defect occurs in production that leads to a (severe) system malfunction causing business to be interrupted for a certain amount of time. • It is associated to the software release in production and, therefore, indirectly to the QoS of QSF for this release. • There are two alternatives for this KPI: either the absolute number of defects leading to business disruption or the residual error rate (calculated to one decimal place and rounded according to the common business rule). The residual error rate is the number of all errors found in validation, verification and production during the first month after go-live divided by the sum of errors found during validation and verification. This involves counting of blocking and serious errors.

Table 6.8 Service Level Agreements

SLA-ID	Level	KQI/KPI	Description	Penalties
SLA-01	QSR	KQI-01	• A QSR meets its service level if the corresponding plan is satisfied. • The measurement is performed and reported every month. • Fulfilment is checked every three months at the end of a quarter.	Penalties are defined in the corresponding contract.
SLA-02	QSF	KPI-01	• On request and after acceptance of the QSR the corresponding V&V orders are executed based on certain preconditions. • Cause and effect of any business disruption are not easily recognisable; therefore the company and the QSF provider need to work together on improving the quality of software releases and processes. • The measurement is performed and reported four weeks after go-live of the corresponding release. • An overall performance appraisal is performed once a year.	Penalties are defined in the corresponding contract.

organisational layers, i.e., the strategic layer, the tactical layer, and the operational layer (cf. Table 6.9).

Table 6.9 Governance Model

	Strategic Layer	Tactical Layer	Operational Layer
Tasks	Coordination and specification of strategic ICT and business guidelines with impact on quality assurance and testing services • Relationship review • Strategic planning	• Executive Steering Committees • Escalation management • Approval for next implementation phase • Ramp up/down • Long-term know-how management according to the release planning • Review transition and onsite / offshore ratio • Periodic reporting	• QSR Management • QSO Management • Review of current testing activities and issues • Planning, monitoring and control • Coordination of testing activities and day-to-day business • KPI / KQI / SLA reporting on service delivery
Governance Level	• Software Prioritisation Committee • Software Customer Council	• Quality Governance • Supplier Governance	• QSR Management • QSO Management
QSF Provider Representative	• Global Account Manager	• Account Manager	• QSF Lead • QSR Manager

The following escalation matrix has been defined to deal with the eventuality of major problems during the operation of a QSF. Reasons which could cause an escalation are:

• A particular service cannot be executed;
• A particular service level cannot be held;
• The quality of results of a certain service is not satisfactory;
• A certain employee has to be replaced.

Two types of escalations are distinguished: horizontal and vertical. If a problem occurs the responsible person is first asked to solve the problem in his specific context. If this is not successful he escalates this to the level indicated in Fig. 6.7.

For example, if a certain quality gate cannot be met during services execution an escalation has to be raised by the QSR Manager. If it is not possible to solve the problem at this level a further escalation has to be raised to the upper level, i.e., the QSF Lead, respectively. Again, if the problem cannot be solved an escalation will

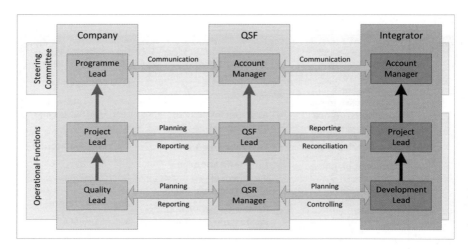

Fig. 6.7   Collaboration and escalation

be raised to the steering committee at management level. If another reason for escalation occurs that is not mentioned here, the defined escalation matrix will also be applied.

Engagement Model and Pricing

The engagement model and pricing are based on the Quality Service Request as well as on the QSF rollout phase.

During the setup phase all prices are based on "Time and Material". Depending on the current client situation and the information within the project, a fixed price can be committed based on a blended rate, including a transparent risk add-on.

Asset and value-based pricing is defined in the execution phase. All activities performed by the QSF will be initiated by a V&V order. Each V&V order then consists of only one service so that the pricing can be related to the assets and values associated with such a service. Table 6.8 is built up from those elements where assets/values come from the service descriptions.

Alternatively, the company can also opt for a blended rate model. However, no rate reduction can be offered in the blended rate model. During the steady-state phase only risk and value-based pricing is defined. Table 6.10 takes the services from Table 6.2 and associates a pricing type.

Table 6.10 Sample pricing configuration of QSF orders during steady-state phase

SID	Service Name	Main Results	Pricing Steady State
QSF-COR -S01	Requirements Analysis with Quality Feedback along the Quality Model ReqQMod	Requirements Quality Report	Package price
QSF-COR -S02	Functional Design Analysis with Quality Feedback along the Quality Model DocQMod	Design Quality Report	Package price
QSF-COR -S03	Architecture Analysis with Quality Feedback along the Quality Model ArchQMod	Architecture Quality Report	Package price
QSF-COR -S04	Code Analysis with Quality Feedback along the Quality Models CodeQMod and DataQMod	Code Quality Report / Data Quality Report	Package price
QSF-COR -S05	Generation of Quality-Ware with Quality Feedback along the defined Quality Models	First version of the respective Quality-Ware	– Not applicable –
QSF-COR -S06	Maintenance of Quality-Ware	New version of the respective Quality-Ware	Package price
QSF-COR -S07	Quality Asset Optimisation	Optimised Quality Assets	Package price
QSF-COR -S08	Product testing	Test Assets for the respective Product	Package price
QSF-COR -S09	Business Process Testing	Test Assets for the respective Business Processes	Package price
QSF-COR -S10	Functional Testing	Test Assets for the respective Functions of an Application	Package price
QSF-COR -S11	Explorative Testing	Test Assets for the respective Test Items	– Not applicable –
QSF-COR -S12	Load/Performance Testing	Test Assets for the respective Test Items	– Not applicable –
QSF-COR -S13	Security Testing	Test Assets for the respective Test Items	– Not applicable –
QSF-COR -S14	Re-Test of Defects along the corresponding Quality Model and Defect List	Test Assets for the respective Test Items	Package price
QSF-MAN-S15	Test Management	Planning, monitoring and control of Testing Activities	– Included in the respective package price –
QSF-MAN-S16	Order Management	Planning, monitoring and control of Orders	– Included in the respective package price –
QSF-MAN-S17	Defect Management	Planning, monitoring and control of Defects	– Included in the respective package price –
QSF-SUP-S18	Test Tool Setup, Maintenance and Operation	Test Tools ready for use	Package price
QSF-SUP-S19	Infrastructure and Environment Management	Infrastructure and Environment ready for use	Package price
QSF-SUP-S20	Test Data Management	Definition, Setup and Maintenance of Test Data	Package price

6.2   Cooperation with Business and ICT

For the success of a QSF it is necessary to define a suitable governance structure and cooperation model between QSF and other organisational units of business and ICT so that all partners have transparency about their responsibilities. Besides a suitable communication structure, the basic principle is defined by gates (cf. Chap. 2).

Table 6.11 Sample quality gates of a QSF

QG	Relevant Artefacts	Quality Criteria	Delivery by Project	Delivery by QSF	Acceptance by Project	Acceptance by QSF	Time for Acceptance
Ready for system test (ST)	Time Schedule - Build for ST	Complete; Consistent; Realisable based on known Operational Risks;	x			x	1
	Report Component Test	Code Coverage (100%);	x			x	2
	Report Component Integration Test	Code Coverage (100%);	x			x	2
	ST Environment	Complete, including Software and Test Data;	x			x	5
	ST Time Schedule	Complete; Consistent; Realisable based on known Operational Risks;		x	x		1
	ST Test Case Specification	Complete, e.g., at least one Concrete Test Case for every Logical Test Case;		x	x		5
	ST Report (including ST results)	Functional Coverage (100%); Test Cases passed (95%);		x	x		3
Ready for acceptance test (UAT)	Time Schedule - Build for UAT	Complete; Consistent; Realisable based on known Operational Risks;	x			x	1
	ST Report	provided by ST					
	UAT Environment	Complete including Software and Test Data;	x			x	5
	UAT Time Schedule	Complete; Consistent; Realisable based on known Operational Risks;		x	x		1
	UAT Test Case Specification (FSpec)	Functional Suitability, e.g., at least one Test Case for every E2E Business Process;		x	x		5
	UAT Test Case Specification (NFSpec)	Performance Efficiency Measure (dependent on Type of Application/System); Reliability Measure (dependent on Type of Application/System); Security Measure (dependent on Potential Threat);		x	x		5
	UAT Report (including UAT Results)	E2E Coverage (100%) and Test Cases passed (95%) and no Critical Incidents; Performance Efficiency Measure (dependent on Type of Application/System); Reliability Measure (dependent on Type of Application/System); Security Measure (dependent on Potential Threat);		x	x		3
Ready for Go-live (GoL)	Time Schedule - Build for Go-live	Complete; Consistent; Realisable based on known Operational Risks;	x				
	UAT Report	Provided by UAT					
	Production Environment	Complete including Software and Production Data;	x				
	Dress Rehearsal	No Critical Incidents and no Risks without Business Continuity Plan;	x				
	Final Acceptance Report (including Dress Rehearsal Results)	Complete in terms of Quality/Risk Directives and Results; Final Recommendation for Go-live.	x				

Quality gates for a certain QSF have to be defined in the QSF concept in the setup phase. Orientation is provided by our lifecycle model (cf. Fig. 6.5).

Quality gates are not only part of the transition between two phases but they can also be placed within a phase. In Table 6.11, we have depicted three examples of quality gates to show useful instantiations from our projects and experiences. The first one is called "Ready for system test", which is needed to verify whether the application or system has the required product properties; the second one is called "Ready for acceptance test", where the potential users verify the quality-in-use

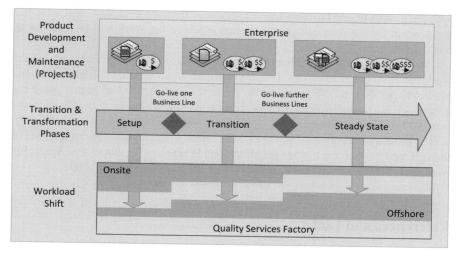

Fig. 6.8 Transition to a QSF

properties of the application and indicate their acceptance; and the last one is called "Ready for go-live", which is usually the last step before the application is handed over to operations. The last QG is a special one because QSF does not participate actively in this QG, but it is mentioned for the sake of completeness and to show how results are used from previous QSF services.

In Table 6.11, the last column is denoted by "time of acceptance", which is measured in working days (WD).

6.3 Transition and Transformation

The approval of a new client follows the strategic planning of the corresponding application implementation. After a positive decision for a new client different phases are distinguished to get this client into the normal QSF operation. The services applied as well as the different QSF implementation stages are schematically presented in Fig. 6.8.

As soon as a new client has been approved the corresponding activities and artefacts will be gradually integrated into the QSF approach. This process is separated into the following three phases:

- Phase 1: Setup;
- Phase 2: Transition;
- Phase 3: Steady State.

Phase 1 (Setup) analyses the current situation at the new client site to find the right strategy and concept for integration in QSF and its services. This phase ends with the go-live of one business line. Experiences from the first phase will influence the concept for the next two phases. A major part of the work will be done by an onsite team.

The next phase, Phase 2 (Execution), is intended to shift a certain amount of the workload from onsite to offsite. This is a continuous process that will give more and more reliance on the QSF approach for the new client. At the end of this phase the go-live of all business lines will be completed. Experiences will influence the concept for the next phase.

The third and last phase, Phase 3 (Steady State), is the normal operating phase of the QSF and its sourcing centres for all upcoming releases for that client. Again, the workload is shifted from onsite to offshore at the highest possible level.

References and Links

Kasmalkar G (2012) Maintenance phase testing—the significant value in doing it right. In: Presentation at QUEST conference on new technologies and methods in quality engineered software and testing, April 30–May 4, 2012, Chicago

Chapter 7
The Benefit of RiSSQ, Balancing Quality and Risk

Remember from Chap. 4 that coincidental quality is free, as it is built into the product by product development and maintenance. If we ask product development and maintenance for the right level of quality or, respectively, risk, it is most often not easy to get insightful and comprehensive answers. However, we still need transparency about quality and risk to be sure that investments into resources (people, money, time, etc.) are sustainable. Ultimately, we need trustworthiness of our ICT landscape and its components.

Quality or, respectively, risk must be predicted and controlled. In the case of quality it is an investment into the future to mitigate business disruption, and in the case of risk it is the costs when risks become losses. Risks can only be managed if they are known. Therefore, investing insufficiently in quality management and quality engineering will lead to substantial costs afterwards. The goal is to balance investments for quality management and engineering with costs for disruptions and losses.

With our notion of right quality we can make transparent what the risks are and where they lie, but also calculate a kind of optimum where investments and residual risks are balanced. This will be described briefly in this chapter.

7.1 Getting Transparency About ICT Product Risks

Quality and risk of an ICT product are two different sides of the same coin. As discussed in Chap. 3, quality is the degree to which a product satisfies the stated and implied needs of its various stakeholders and thus provides value to the enterprise. In contrast, risk is the degree to which a product does not satisfy the stated and implied needs of its various stakeholders and thus represents potential damages and losses. Risk changes over time and depending on the stakeholders, as does quality (cf. Chaps. 2 and 3). What does this mean for an ICT product during its lifecycle? Let us briefly discuss current reasoning in enterprises based on Fig. 7.1.

M. Wieczorek et al., *Systems and Software Quality*,
DOI 10.1007/978-3-642-39971-8_7, © Springer-Verlag Berlin Heidelberg 2014

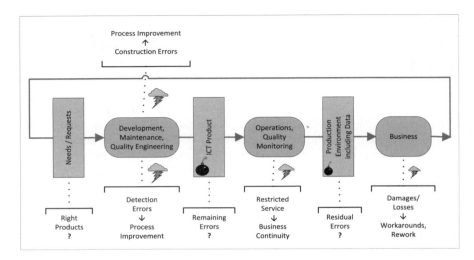

Fig. 7.1 Quality and risk evolution

The process starts with the needs or requests from the business for new or modified functionality or improved efficiency. Most often this leads to the development of a new ICT product or to the modification of an existing one (maintenance). When the product has been completed Operations moves it into the production environment. Once this has all been finalised, hopefully business is satisfied with the solution.

During the various stages there is the potential of making errors, wrong or inappropriate decisions and delivering solutions that are cumbersome and error-prone. Two questions need to be answered; are the processes right and are the intermediate products right? Assuming that the needs or requests are described in a suitable way—which unfortunately is not always the case—development or maintenance and quality engineering start their construction and detection processes. This stage in Fig. 7.1 is error-prone in the sense that errors might be generated during construction and errors might be generated during detection of construction errors. Processes and artefacts in subsequent stages of the lifecycle depend, to a varying extent, on processes and artefacts in earlier stages of the lifecycle. Appropriate methods, procedures and tools need to be applied during error detection to get transparency about the quality or risk of such processes and artefacts. Naturally, this is also valid for the final product. At the end of each process we know there will not be 100 % quality nor will there be 0 % risk in the intermediate artefacts and the final ICT product. There will be residual errors when going live, but most often we do not know what they are. What we need is a prediction about the quality level or, respectively, the risk level. The latter seems easier to calculate because we already have many methods from risk management.

The next stage in Fig. 7.1 is "operations and quality monitoring". Operations must provide mechanisms to ensure business continuity in case of failing application or systems. Therefore, it would also be necessary to align the quality or risk level coming from development or maintenance to the needs of business continuity (cf. Wieczorek et al. 2002). At the end of this process, Operations provides a production environment which business applies in daily work. So, quality emerges during development and maintenance and must be made transparent for the relevant stakeholders, the C-level, the senior management and at the operational layer to deliver trustworthy ICT solutions and products to the business.

To get transparency about the risk level and the investments for all the artefacts in the lifecycle it is worthwhile having a calculation mechanism that helps to take the right decisions about quality and risk levels and investments. Remember the different lifecycle phases and their artefacts in Chap. 2:

1. Identification of needs—a sample artefact is the "needs documentation";
2. Definition of project scope and planning—a sample artefact is the "project charter";
3. Requirements analysis—a sample artefact is the "requirements specification";
4. Functional and technical design—a sample artefact is the "architecture model";
5. Development—a sample artefact is the "source code";
6. Integration and testing—a sample artefact is the "system cluster";
7. Implementation—a sample artefact is the "system landscape";
8. Operations & maintenance—a sample artefact is the productive system (ICT landscape).

For all relevant artefacts it is necessary to answer the following questions to predict the quality and risk level and to compare this with targets coming from the tactical and strategic layers in an enterprise. This is also needed to align investments for quality assurance with ICT strategy.

1. What is the risk delivered by an unverified architecture model based on current development methods, procedures, and resources without error detection?
2. Which additional investment is needed for error detection?
3. Which methods are available for error detection?
4. What is the additional effort for supplementary error detection activities?
5. What is the expected risk reduction of supplementary error detection activities?

The sample sheet in Fig. 7.2 will help to analyse the situation in an enterprise when starting a project or for strategic reasons. The relevant artefacts are set out in relation to the parameters to be filled in.

In conclusion, we need a calculation method that allows for reasoning about quality or risk during the whole lifecycle, which then allows for acceptance criteria in intermediate quality gates and during acceptance of the final product and provides suggestions for business continuity in operations.

	Expected Risk	Risk Reduction	Investment	Time Schedule	Remaining Risk
Needs Documentation					
Project Documentation					
Requirements					
Architecture		1. Calculation by experts			
Source Code		2. Simulation of different scenarios			
Product/System		3. Decision about scenario to be taken			
System Cluster					
ICT Systems Landscape					

Fig. 7.2 RiSSQ calculation sheet

- 0% Transparency
- Coincidental Quality

→ not acceptable

RiSSQ
Right Software and Systems Quality

→ acceptable and affordable

- 100% Transparency
- Maximum Quality

→ not affordable

Fig. 7.3 Balancing quality and risk

7.2   Balancing Quality and Risk

As already discussed in previous chapters, direct measures for quality are difficult
to define and most often we find substitutes approximating in some sense the
quality. This is not the case with the other two important indicators of projects,
namely budget and time. There is other work that also deals with measurement and
control of software product quality, e.g. Wagner (2013) and Boland et al. (2010).
What is needed is a balancing of quality and risk as portrayed in Fig. 7.3.

In Chap. 3 we introduced our notion of Right Software and Systems Quality.
This notion relates the investments for the verification and validation of particular
quality characteristics to budget and time. We will use our RiSSQ calculation
method to demonstrate an example taken from verification of a particular ICT
system (product). Our calculation method needs various input data for calibration
and predicts the risk level and the investment and as such produces different
scenarios to get the right quality/risk level. Various input parameters are required
for the calculations, e.g.

- Target values;
- V&V calibration values; and
- Project classification value.

A simplified representation of such a calculation is provided in Fig. 7.4. The two
diagrams in Fig. 7.5 show the same value of the sheet in graphical format. It gives
an overview of where to invest and what the expected risk level is.

			Functional Testing	Functional Regression Testing	Performance Testing	Security Testing	Business Process Testing	Total
	V&V Procedures		FT	FRT	PT	ST	BPT	T
V&V Calibration	Normalised Effort	[unit]	0.75	0.25	2.50	2.50	1.25	
	Hit Rate	[%]	90.00%	90.00%	60.00%	80.00%	90.00%	
Project Classification	System Risk due to Change Request	Index	100	30	20	60	50	260
		[%]	38.46%	11.54%	7.69%	23.08%	19.23%	100.00%
	V&V Volume	Units	500	500	15	50	50	
	Affected Volume	[%]	30.00%	70.00%	80.00%	10.00%	100.00%	
Prediction for V&V	Risk Reduction	Index	90	27	12	48	45	222
		[%]	40.54%	12.16%	5.41%	21.62%	20.27%	100.00%
	Residual Risk	Index	10	3	8	12	5	38
		[%]	3.85%	1.15%	3.08%	4.62%	1.92%	14.62%
	Investment	[€/unit]	750 €	750 €	900 €	1000 €	850 €	
		[€]	84,375 €	65,625 €	27,000 €	12,500 €	53,125 €	242,625 €
		[%]	34.78%	27.05%	11.12%	5.15%	21.90%	100.00%

Calculation Scenario for a particular Change Request

Target / Prediction
Residual Risk Level: 20.00% / 14.62%
Investment for QA: 180,000 € / 242,625 €

Fig. 7.4 Sample RiSSQ calculation for a change request

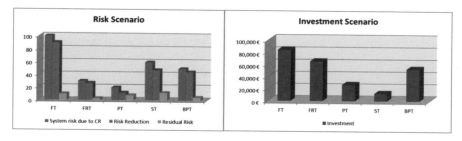

Fig. 7.5 Investment/risk diagrams for sample RiSSQ calculation

References and Links

Boland T, Cleraux C, Fong E (2010) Toward a preliminary framework for assessing the trustworthiness of software. Software and Systems Division, Information Technology Laboratory, NIST National Institute of Standards and Technology, Gaithersburg, MD

Wagner S (2013) Software product quality control. Springer, Berlin

Wieczorek M, Naujoks U, Bartlett B (eds) (2002) Business continuity—IT risk management for international corporations. Springer, Berlin

Chapter 8
Summary and Conclusion

This chapter concludes our journey through an enterprise, in which we examined ICT and quality aspects and discussed our holistic approach to enterprise-wide ICT quality. To this end we defined and discussed three pillars: a fundamental notion of Right Software and Systems Quality; portfolio management, quality governance, quality management, and quality engineering as a holistic approach across the three layers of en enterprise, i.e. strategic, tactical, and operational; and an industrialisation framework for implementing quality engineering.

Section 8.1 describes what we have achieved in chapters one to seven of this book and Sect. 8.2 provides a checklist for establishing our approach in an enterprise.

8.1 What Has Been Achieved

During the writing of this book many faults and failures occurred in real systems where technology, software, and people played a significant role, where uncertainties about the real properties of the respective systems were recognised, and where it was not known how much to invest in quality engineering to reach a particular residual risk level. Take the following example, translated from Burkert (2013):

> "Many popular Android-based Apps have severe security problems. This is not just annoying but could lead to significant damages, because banks and publishers also use them. Android is the de facto mobile operating system. It is installed worldwide on the majority of mobile devices like Smartphones and Tablets"

Sandberg and Rollins also state in their book (Sandberg and Rollins 2013)

> "If you want to reach the most users with a single code base, Android is the way"

Based on such examples we have argued in this book that the two worlds of ICT systems and embedded systems are coming together, that the software industry is on

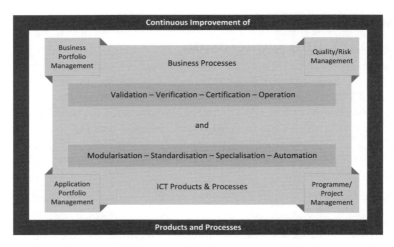

Fig. 8.1 Enterprise ICT Quality enabling RiSSQ

the verge of industrialising its development processes, and that quality management and quality engineering therefore have to be revisited.

We started from the premise of focusing more on ICT products and their lifecycles rather than thinking purely in terms of projects. Furthermore, we argued that it takes more than just better methods, procedures and tools as part of quality management and quality engineering to improve the quality of ICT products and to ensure business quality. An integrated, holistic approach to quality issues in all their manifestations must be established and implemented in an enterprise. In doing so, the industrialisation of quality engineering will also be a matter of choice as will the integration with portfolio management.

We have discussed and defined three pillars in this book:

1. A fundamental notion of Right Software and Systems Quality;
2. A management approach consisting of portfolio management, risk management, quality governance and quality management addressing all three layers of an enterprise, i.e. strategic, tactical and operational;
3. An industrialisation framework for implementing RiSSQ in an enterprise.

The cornerstones of our approach are depicted in Fig. 8.1.

Chapter 1: Motivation and Introduction

As a relatively young industry, the software industry has for many years sought new methods, procedures, and tools to make software development less error-prone and more cost-effective. A lot of new paradigms have been invented, such as incremental and Agile development paradigms. Product quality and process quality have become equally important concepts. All in all, we believe that a next step is necessary to improve software development, or parts of it, in the broader sense.

We discussed examples from several publications of cases where software-based systems failed. A brief history of ICT systems and embedded systems was presented for comparison reasons. We analysed similarities and differences between the ICT world and the embedded world to learn from both worlds and to enable improvements of ICT systems quality. We discussed the main challenges in the lifecycle of software-based systems and revisited existing industrialisation approaches.

To conclude the first chapter we postulated a holistic quality approach consisting of three pillars:

1. An enterprise-wide concept integrating portfolio management, quality governance, quality and risk management, and quality engineering;
2. An industrialisation model for quality engineering as implementation framework; and
3. An enterprise-wide notion of a right level of software and systems quality.

Chapter 2: The Four "P"s of Enterprise ICT

A holistic quality approach is founded on a certain view on enterprises and their ICT. Characterising enterprises and their ICT is a complex task and many disciplines and people have done excellent work on it. It is not our goal here to provide another theory of Business Administration, Computer Science, ICT Management or the like, but rather to present a holistic approach for quality issues that are vertically and horizontally aligned with the enterprise's organisation.

Such an approach must be aligned with business demands and affects the people that work there, the implemented processes, the implemented ICT products and applications, and the defined ICT programmes and projects. We have discussed all these topics and called them the four "P"s of enterprise ICT, where the four "P"s indicate (1) People, (2) Processes, (3) Products, and (4) Projects and Portfolio.

Chapter 3: What Is Right Software and Systems Quality?

Of course, the software industry has accepted that quality of software-based systems is important. A variety of tools have been made available to conduct computer aided verification and validation of the respective artefacts. Most of them are dedicated to dynamic testing and static code quality control. The tools themselves cover an array of testing capabilities, and span the dynamics of various scenarios across projects and application development environments through production systems. Usually, projects or programmes are initiated to enhance, replace, maintain or improve software-based systems. Such projects and programmes have defined goals and frame conditions which are mostly directed to functionality, budget and time. But the question "where do quality requirements come from" is equally important.

We have considered quality characteristics for quality-in-use and product quality based on the ISO standard series (cf. ISO/IEC 25010 2011 and ISO/IEC 25012 2008) and provided, from practice, an evaluation of the relevance of particular quality characteristics for several system types, e.g. legacy systems. We also challenged different stakeholders and their expectations regarding quality characteristics. This led us directly to the discussion "do properties of software-based systems change over time and in response to changing stakeholder's expectations". Furthermore, we defined our notion of Right Software and Systems Quality and suggested a practicable quality model for each lifecycle artefact.

Chapter 4: How Can We Establish Right Quality for an Enterprise?

In 2012, ISACA published results from a survey of over 3,700 global business and ICT professionals and members of ISACA (2012). More than 40 % worked in organisations in the finance, banking, insurance, government and military sectors. One surprising result was that more than 50 % of respondents indicated "business management's level of involvement in the governance of enterprise ICT is not very high".

In our view, it is time in the ICT world to take a product-oriented approach as well as a project-oriented approach. ICT systems are products, so there are two important issues to consider; ensuring it is the right product and guaranteeing that the product has the right quality. Clear goals from the top management are needed which set the scope and freedom for actions but also for quality characteristics. We therefore discussed our concept of integrated portfolio management, quality governance and quality management aimed at all three layers of an enterprise, i.e. the strategic, the tactical and the operational. Each enterprise layer has been described individually.

Chapter 5: How Can We Implement a Framework for Right Quality?

To create a framework for right quality that enables full transparency about the quality of products and alignment of risks with the business needs of the enterprise means to implement a holistic and integrated quality approach. In our view, this approach must be both product and process oriented. Our framework for enabling right quality accompanies organisations on their journey from relying completely on individually acting people to a highly efficient and profitable Quality Services Factory characterised by an adequate degree of industrialisation that focuses on quality engineering.

The most suitable way of evaluating and improving organisations through industrialisation is to successively implement the five dimensions of our "House of Quality". These dimensions are modularisation, standardisation, specialisation, automation and continuous improvement supported by quality management and quality governance. The order in which this is done should be considered thoroughly; otherwise, it could lead to a revision of the complete quality engineering approach. The highest leverage effect can be reached by generally following the sequence above, even if it is possible and sometimes necessary to work in parallel on selected issues of different dimensions for local improvements or to mitigate high priority risks. For example, automation of particular quality aspects is most efficient when modularisation and standardisation have already been implemented to a certain extent to avoid redundant work and maintenance. Additionally, this order gives a high degree of reuse of pre-existing components.

Chapter 6: The Quality Services Factory

An increasing number of companies across various industries have implemented an internal shared-services model that delivers ICT services to their end users or customers. The objective of the shared-services team is to drive enhancements and improvements of the existing business applications and operating systems. In addition, they focus on the consolidation and replacement of legacy systems that are the result of acquisitions or have been accumulated over time as part of the overall operating system.

We are convinced that a holistic approach, focused on ICT quality, which combines product orientation with industrialised quality engineering and a sound notion of right quality will reduce costs. The ultimate goal of industrialisation as discussed in Chap. 5 is the so-called Quality Services Factory. It is helpful to align with a strategic partner to define, build and operate such a model. There are several reasons to involve a specialist, specifically acceleration of model implementation, experience, best practices, independence and flexibility. The receiving organisation can bring knowledge and experiences in their own domain and methodologies. The specialist organisation can bring many years of experiences in implementing and improving the necessary processes of a wide array of customers.

Transforming a current quality organisation into a QSF requires various aspects and tasks to be considered upfront. This is independent of whether the QSF is operated completely internally or in collaboration with a strategic partner. Various aspects and tasks have been discussed, such as QSF services, QSF processes and structures, QSF escalation mechanisms and the QSF cooperation model with business and other ICT organisations in the company.

Chapter 7: The Benefit of RiSSQ, Balancing Quality and Risk

In Chap. 4 we argued that coincidental quality is free, as it is built into the product by product development and maintenance. If we ask product development and maintenance for the right level of quality or, respectively, risk, it is not easy to get insightful and comprehensive answers. However, we still need transparency about quality and risk to be sure that investments into resources (people, money, time, etc.) are sustainable. Ultimately, we need trustworthiness of our ICT landscape and its components.

Quality or, respectively, risk must be predicted and controlled. In the case of quality it is an investment in the future to mitigate business disruption, and in the case of risk it is the costs when risks become losses. Risks can only be managed if they are known. Therefore, investing insufficiently in quality management and quality engineering will lead to costs that could have been avoided. The goal is to balance investments for quality management and quality engineering with costs for disruptions and losses. We argued that with our notion of RiSSQ we can make transparent what the risks are and where they lie, but also calculate a kind of optimum where investments and residual risks are balanced.

8.2   A Checklist for Establishing RiSSQ in an Enterprise

We will conclude this chapter with a checklist for establishing RiSSQ in an enterprise or whether organisations have a sound and comprehensive portfolio management and quality governance system in place. We have divided the checklist into three separate tables: Table 8.1 concerns the strategic layer, Table 8.2 applies to the tactical layer, and Table 8.3 applies to the operational layer.

Table 8.1 Checklist—Strategic Layer

	Topics	Questions
Strategic Layer	Portfolio Management	1. Do you regularly evaluate changes in your business and markets?
		2. Do you have a portfolio management process?
		3. Do you have a defined business portfolio?
		4. Do you have a business process architecture?
		5. Are you making the right investments? Do you have defined assessment criteria?
		6. Are you confident that the chosen programmes and projects will be delivered well and meet their strategic goals? Do you have defined assessment criteria?
		7. Do you trust that the organisation is operating in order to realise the expected values? Do you have defined assessment criteria?
	Quality Risk Model	1. Do you have a strategic quality risk model at enterprise level (policies, needs, risks and quality characteristics)?
		2. Do you regularly take into account changes in business and stakeholder expectations for the quality risk model?
		3. Do you have standardised KQIs and KPIs?
		4. Do you have an implementation plan for the quality risk model as a directive for the tactical layer?
		5. Can you manage the quality of your ICT landscape according to defined KQIs and KPIs?
	Directives and Feedback Loop	1. Do you have a defined enterprise and ICT governance structure?
		2. Do you have a defined quality governance structure?
		3. Do you have assigned quality governance goals and responsibilities?
		4. Do you provide directives to the tactical layer concerning programmes and their quality and risk goals?
		5. Do you have a communication and training concept for the quality governance framework?
		6. Do you have a regular management review process to analyse feedback and to communicate and agree on corrective actions?
		7. Do you have a systematic approach to collect and retain goals, measurements and evaluation results?
		8. Is there a feedback loop from the tactical to the strategic layer?

Table 8.2 Checklist—Tactical Layer

	Topics	Questions
Tactical Layer	Portfolio Management	1. Are you doing the right programmes and projects according to the investment decisions at the strategic layer?
		2. Do you have a defined application portfolio?
		3. Do you have the right application landscape for your business needs?
		4. Are you confident that all applications support your business in all its forms?
		5. Do you know whether all applications have the right quality? Do you have defined assessment criteria?
		6. Do you know whether the investments in applications are related to the risk level of that application? Do you have defined assessment criteria?
		7. Do you have defined industrialisation goals? Do you have defined assessment criteria?
	Quality Risk Models for Systems and Applications	1. Do you have a quality risk model for every application or system? Do you have defined assessment criteria?
		2. Do you take into account the different domains and business processes for the quality risk model definition?
		3. Do the quality risk models satisfy the strategic directives?
		4. Do you have a defined quality risk model for all relevant artefacts of the established processes of programmes and projects?
		5. Do you have defined verification and validation assets for the various applications or systems due to the quality risk models?
		6. Do you have defined verification and validation assets for the various business processes in connection with the quality risk models?
	V&V Assets for Systems and Applications	1. Do you have defined and established standards for verification and validation assets that are to be used in the programmes and projects?
		2. Do you have an industrialisation framework? Do you have defined assessment criteria?
		3. Do you have an infrastructure framework for verification and validation, including standard environments, tools and procedures?
		4. Do you have defined criteria for building a regression framework, e.g. verification and validation rules?
		5. Do you have a framework for retaining quality assets?
		6. Are you confident that the quality assets are reused by the programmes and projects? Do you have defined assessment criteria?
	Directives and Feedback Loop	1. Do you know the directives from the strategic layer?
		2. Are you confident that quality management has the right responsibilities to align the quality demands to strategic goals? Do you have defined assessment criteria?
		3. Do you collect, retain and analyse data in compliance with the quality governance directives?
		4. Do you have regular mechanisms to evaluate data, feedback and satisfaction of defined directives? Do you have defined assessment criteria?
		5. Is there any feedback loop from the operational to the tactical layer?

Table 8.3 Checklist—Operational Layer

	Topics		Questions
Operational Layer	Quality Requirements and Risk Mitigation	1.	Do you have detailed regulations and criteria to evaluate risks at the operational layer (programmes/projects, applications/systems)?
		2.	Do you have the derived quality criteria and risk mitigation plans systematically checked against actual review results and released afterwards?
		3.	Is the coverage of quality goals and criteria evaluated as part of the sign off process?
		4.	Do the projects get their quality requirements from the tactical layer?
	V&V Assets in Projects	1.	Do the projects get the verification and validation assets from the tactical layer?
		2.	Do you have a defined regression test frame that is derived from the standard asset library?
		3.	Do the projects make use of standard assets for the verification and validation of artefacts?
	Lessons learned and Feedback Loop	1.	Is there a feedback loop from the operational to the tactical to the strategic layer for monitoring and control of quality and risk?
		2.	Is there an experience database to collect and evaluate the KQI and KPI data provided by operations and maintenance?
		3.	Is there a list of selected tasks derived from Quality Management standards and/or lessons learned from previous projects?
		4.	Is there a summary of evaluated lessons learned, prepared from current projects?

References and Links

Burkert A (2013) Systemterror durch fehlerhafte Apps für Android. Redaktion Springer für Professionals. Published 10.12.2013. Retrieved 21 Jan 2014

ISACA (2012) Governance of enterprise IT (GEIT) survey—global edition. http://www.isaca.org/Pages/2012-Governance-of-Enterprise-IT-GEIT-Survey.aspx. Retrieved 11 Nov 2013

ISO/IEC 25010 (2011) Systems and software engineering—systems and software quality requirements and evaluation (SQuaRE)—system and software quality models. International Organization for Standardization (ISO), Geneva

ISO/IEC 25012 (2008) Software engineering—software product quality requirements and evaluation (SQuaRE)—Data quality model. International Organization for Standardization (ISO), Geneva

Sandberg R, Rollins M (2013) The business of Android apps development: making and marketing apps that succeed on Google Play, Amazon Appstore and more. Apress, New York, NY

Appendix A: Quality Models and Verification Methods

As indicated in previous chapters, we have excluded discussions on the various verification methods which still exist in many publications. The following table may be useful in researching appropriate methods to deal with the different artefacts in the product lifecycle. We do not claim completeness in the methods but have provided common verification methods which we apply in our projects.

Artefact type	Quality model	Verification methods
Documentation	DocQMod	• Peer Review • Structured Group Review • Inspection • Walk Through • Technical Review • Informal Review
Business processes	BPQMod	• Peer Review • Structured Group Review • Formal Inspection (on business process models, e.g. swimlanes, business and application process models) • Walk Through • GUI Prototyping • Test Modelling (based on business processes) • Early Test Case Design • Usability Testing
Requirements	ReqQMod	• Management Review • Peer Review • Structured Group Review • Audit • Inspection • Walk Through • Technical Review • Informal review • GUI Prototyping • Test Modelling (based on requirements) • Test Case Specification (based on requirements)

(continued)

M. Wieczorek et al., *Systems and Software Quality*,
DOI 10.1007/978-3-642-39971-8, © Springer-Verlag Berlin Heidelberg 2014

Artefact type	Quality model	Verification methods
Architecture	ArchQMod	• Peer Review • Structured Group Review • Formal Inspection • ATAM • Prototyping (including functional and non-functional testing) • FMEA
Database	DataQMod	• Formal Inspection (on e.g. normalisation) • Peer Review (on indexing, SQL statements, stored procedures) • Structured Group Review • Functional Testing (by application) • Non-functional testing (including performance and security)
Source code	CodeQMod	• Peer Review • Walk Through • Formal Inspection (e.g. style guides, coding standards) • Static Source Code Analysis (tool based) • Profiling (e.g. memory leaks) • Functional and Non-Functional dynamic testing • Condition Testing • Branch Testing • LCSAJ Testing
(Parts of) application or system	SysQMod	• Business Process Testing • End-to-End Testing • Functional Testing • Non-Functional Testing (e.g. reliability, performance, security, and usability testing) • Structure-based Testing • Specification-based Testing • Testing using Decision Tables • Testing using State Transition Diagrams • Testing using Equivalence Partitioning • Boundary Value Analysis • Cause-Effect Graphing • Combinatorial Testing • Use Case Testing • User Story Testing • Domain Analysis • Explorative Testing • Crowd Testing • Manual / Automated Testing
Environment	EnvQMod	• Peer Review • Structured Group Review • Formal Inspection • ATAM • Prototyping (including functional and non-functional testing) • FMEA • Monitoring • In-Process Reviews

(continued)

Artefact type	Quality model	Verification methods
Long-term archive	DigPresQMod	• Inspection • Peer Review • Recoverability Testing • Regression Testing • Inspections by Samples • Spot Test

Appendix B: Relevant International Standards

All standards, quasi-standards or industry-specific standards like DO 178C, AQAP or CMMI are mostly derived from national or international standards developed by various national and international standardisation bodies. In the table below we have limited our scope to the international standards that are relevant for the purposes of this book and focus on quality governance, quality management and quality engineering. If there is a standard that does not apply by country, there should be a relatively close conversion within that country.

Reference number	Title
IEC 31010: 2009	Risk management—Risk assessment techniques
IEEE STD 1028: 2008	IEEE Standard for Software Reviews and Audits
ISO 9000: 2005	Quality management systems—Fundamentals and vocabulary
ISO 9001: 2008	Quality management systems—Requirements
ISO 9004: 2009	Managing for the sustained success of an organization—A quality management approach
ISO 10001: 2007	Quality management—Customer satisfaction—Guidelines for codes of conduct for organizations
ISO 10002: 2009	Quality management—Customer satisfaction—Guidelines for complaints handling in organizations
ISO 10003: 2007	Quality management—Customer satisfaction—Guidelines for dispute resolution external to organizations
ISO 10005: 2005	Quality management systems—Guidelines for quality plans
ISO 10005: 2005	Quality management systems—Guidelines for quality plans
ISO 10006: 2003	Quality management systems—Guidelines for quality management in projects
ISO 10007: 2003	Quality management systems—Guidelines for configuration management
ISO 10012: 2003	Measurement management systems—Requirements for measurement processes and measuring equipment
ISO/TR 10013: 2001	Guidelines for quality management system documentation
ISO 10014: 2007	Quality management—Guidelines for realizing financial and economic benefits
ISO 10014: 2006	Quality management—Guidelines for realizing financial and economic benefits

(continued)

M. Wieczorek et al., *Systems and Software Quality*,
DOI 10.1007/978-3-642-39971-8, © Springer-Verlag Berlin Heidelberg 2014

Reference number	Title
ISO 10015: 1999	Quality management—Guidelines for training
ISO 10018: 2012	Quality management—Guidelines on people involvement and competence
ISO 10019: 2005	Guidelines for the selection of quality management system consultants and use of their service
ISO 19011: 2012	Guidelines for auditing management systems
ISO 26262-1: 2011	Road vehicles—Functional safety—Vocabulary
ISO 26262-2: 2011	Road vehicles—Functional safety—Management of functional safety
ISO 26262-3: 2011	Road vehicles—Functional safety—Concept phase
ISO 26262-4: 2011	Road vehicles—Functional safety—Product development at the system level
ISO 26262-5: 2011	Road vehicles—Functional safety—Product development at the hardware level
ISO 26262-6: 2011	Road vehicles—Functional safety—Product development at the software level
ISO 26262-7: 2011	Road vehicles—Functional safety—Production and operation
ISO 26262-8: 2011	Road vehicles—Functional safety—Supporting processes
ISO 26262-9: 2011	Road vehicles—Functional safety—Automotive Safety Integrity Level (ASIL)oriented and safety-oriented analyses
ISO 26262-10: 2012	Road vehicles—Functional safety—Guideline on ISO 26262
ISO 31000: 2009	Risk management—Principles and guidelines
ISO/IEC 12207: 2008	Systems and software engineering—Software life cycle processes
ISO/IEC 15288: 2008	Systems and software engineering—System life cycle processes
ISO/IEC 15504-1: 2004	Information technology—Process assessment—Part 1: Concepts and vocabulary
ISO/IEC 15504-2: 2003	Information technology—Process assessment—Part 2: Performing an assessment
ISO/IEC 15504-3: 2004	Information technology—Process assessment—Part 3: Guidance on performing an assessment
ISO/IEC 15504-4: 2004	Information technology—Process assessment—Part 4: Guidance on use for process improvement and process capability determination
ISO/IEC 15504-5: 2012	Information technology—Process assessment—An exemplar software life cycle process assessment model
ISO/IEC 15504-7: 2008	Information technology—Process assessment—Part 7: Assessment of organizational maturity
ISO/IEC 15504-9: 2011	Information technology—Process assessment—Part 9: Target process profiles
ISO/IEC 15504-10: 2011	Information technology—Process assessment—Part 10: Safety extension
ISO/IEC 16085: 2006	Systems and software engineering—Life cycle processes—Risk management
ISO/IEC 20000-1: 2011	Information technology—Service management—Part 1: Service management system requirements
ISO/IEC 20000-2: 2012	Information technology—Service management—Part 2: Guidance on the application of service management systems
ISO/IEC 25010: 2011	Systems and Software-Engineering—Systems and software Quality Requirements and Evaluation (SQuaRE)—System and software quality models

(continued)

Reference number	Title
ISO/IEC 25012: 2008	Software-Engineering—Software product Quality Requirements and Evaluation (SQuaRE)—Data quality model
ISO/IEC 25020: 2007	Software-Engineering—Software product Quality Requirements and Evaluation (SQuaRE)—Measurement reference model and guide
ISO/IEC 25021: 2012	Systems and Software-Engineering—Systems and software Quality Requirements and Evaluation (SQuaRE)—Quality measure elements
ISO/IEC 25030: 2007	Software-Engineering—Software product Quality Requirements and Evaluation (SQuaRE)—Quality requirements
ISO/IEC 25040: 2011	Systems and Software-Engineering—Systems and software Quality Requirements and Evaluation (SQuaRE)—Evaluation process
ISO/IEC 25041: 2012	Systems and Software-Engineering—Systems and software Quality Requirements and Evaluation (SQuaRE)—Evaluation guide for developers, acquirers and independent evaluators
ISO/IEC 27001: 2013	Information technology—Security techniques—Information security management systems—Requirements
ISO/IEC 90003: 2004	Software engineering—Guidelines for the application of ISO 9001 to computer software
ISO/IEC FDIS 25000: 2013	Systems and Software-Engineering—Systems and software Quality Requirements and Evaluation (SQuaRE)—Guide to SQuaRE
ISO/IEC FDIS 25001: 2013	Systems and Software-Engineering—Systems and software Quality Requirements and Evaluation (SQuaRE)—Planning and management
ISO/IEC/IEEE 29119-1: 2013	Software and Systems-Engineering—Software-Testing—Concepts and definitions
ISO/IEC/IEEE 29119-2: 2013	Software and Systems-Engineering—Software-Testing—Test process
ISO/IEC/IEEE 29119-3: 2013	Software and Systems-Engineering—Software-Testing—Test documentation
ISO/IEC/IEEE 29148: 2011	Systems and software engineering—Life cycle processes—Requirements engineering

Glossary

AG Aktiengesellschaft; company limited by shares

Agile A group of software development methods based on iterative and incremental development, where requirements and solutions evolve through collaboration between self-organising, cross-functional teams

Anti-pattern Pattern used in social or business operations or software engineering that may be commonly used but is ineffective and/or counterproductive in practice.

APM Application Portfolio Management

AQAP Allied Quality Assurance Publications (of NATO)

ArchQMod Architecture Quality Model

ASP Application Service Providing

Asset Objects or items which can be created and modified

AT&T American Telephone and Telegraph Company

ATAM Architecture Tradeoff Analysis Method

ATM Automated Teller Machine

Avaloq Banking software solution; also the Swiss based company developing the software

Basel II Second of the Basel Accords, which are recommendations on banking laws and regulations issued by the Basel Committee on Banking Supervision

Basel III Third of the Basel Accords, which is a global, voluntary regulatory standard on bank capital adequacy, stress testing and market liquidity risk issued by the Basel Committee on Banking Supervision

BAT Business Acceptance Test

BFSI Banking, Financial Services and Insurance

BMW Bayrische Motorenwerke; a German based car company

BP Business Process

BPM Business Process Management

BPO Business Process Outsourcing

BPQMod Business Process Quality Model

Breadboard Assemblies Standardised procedure for verification and validation of systems or components and for integration of such components

M. Wieczorek et al., *Systems and Software Quality*,
DOI 10.1007/978-3-642-39971-8, © Springer-Verlag Berlin Heidelberg 2014

BSC Balanced Scorecard Collaborative

BU Business Unit

Business disruption Interruption of operations or breakdown

CAN Controller Area Network; bus system for mainstream powertrain communications

CH Channel

CEO Chief Executive Officer

CI Continuous Improvement

CIO Chief Information Officer

Cluster Analysis Cluster analysis or clustering is the task of grouping a set of objects in such a way that objects in the same group (called a cluster) are more similar (in some sense or another) to each other than to those in other groups (clusters)

CMMI Capability Maturity Model Integration

COO Chief Operation Officer

COBIT Control Objectives for Information and Related Technology

COBIT5 A Business Framework for the Governance and Management of Enterprise IT

CodeQMod Code quality model

COR Core Services

CPU Central Processing Units

CR Change Request

CxO either CEO or COO or CIO

DataQMod Data quality model

Deadlock A deadlock is a situation in which two or more competing actions are each waiting for the other to finish, and thus neither ever does

DigPresQMod Digital preservation quality model

DO 178C Industry-specific standard entitled "Software Considerations in Airborne Systems and Equipment Certification" and published by RTCA, Inc., in a joint effort with EUROCAE

DocQMod Documentation Quality Model

DPE Digital Preservation Europe; a EU based organisation

E/E Electric and Electronic

E2E End to End

EAM Enterprise Architecture Management

ECU Electronic Control Unit

EFQM European Foundation for Quality Management Model

EnvQMod Environments Quality Model

ERP Enterprise Resource Planning

EUROCAE European Organisation for Civil Aviation Equipment

ES Embedded System

EU European Union

EW Embedded World

FlexRay Bus system for higher-end applications

FMEA Failure Mode and Effects Analysis

FSpec Test case specification addressing functional properties

GoL Go-live

Go-live A phase at the of software development which turns on the software for users in a productive environment

GUI Graphical User Interface

HiL Hardware in the Loop

HoQ House of Quality

I/O Input/Output

ICT Information and Communication Technology

ICTS Information and Communication Technology System

ICTW Information and Communication Technology World

IEC International Electrotechnical Commission

IEEE Institute of Electrical and Electronics Engineers

IQA Individual Quality Approach

iqnite Conference for Software Quality Management

ISACA Information Systems Audit and Control Association; a US based organisation

ISO International Organization for Standardization

ISTQB International Software Testing Qualifications Board

ITGI IT Governance Institute

ITIL Information Technology Infrastructure Library

IT the two terms IT and ICT will be used as synonyms although our preferred term in this book is ICT

KID Identification number for KPI/KQI

KPI Key Performance Indicator

KQI Key Quality Indicator

LCSAJ Linear Code Sequence And Jump

Legacy system An old computer system or application program

Lifecycle A number of sequential stages grouped together, ranging from its initial idea and development to its eventual disposal, and including updated versions of the released version to help improve software or fix bugs still present in the product

LIN Local Interconnected Network; bus system for lower-cost electronics

Machina Research A technology research and consulting firm, UK based company

MAN Management Services

MS Microsoft

NAF NATO Architecture Framework

NASDAQ National Association of Securities Dealers Automated Quotations; a US based organisation

NATO North Atlantic Treaty Organization

Nearshore Performing a task at the premises of an outsourcing partner but in the same country

NFSpec Test case specification addressing non-functional properties
NHTSA National Highway Traffic Safety Administration; a US based organisation
NYSE New York Stock Exchange; a US based organisation
OEM Original Equipment Manufacturer
Offshore Performing a task at the premises of an outsourcing partner but in a different country
Off-site Performing a task at the company's premises but another location
On-site Performing a task at the company's premises at the same location
OXL Order Execution Line
PMI Project Management Institute
PC Personal computer
PhD Doctor of Philosophy (academic degree)
PLM Product Lifecycle Management
PMO Project Management Office
PPM Project Portfolio Management
PQM Portfolio Quality Management
ProcQMod Process Quality Model
ProdQMod Product Quality Model
QA Quality Assurance
QE Quality Engineering
QG Quality Gate
QGov Quality Governance
QI Quality Intelligence
QiUQMod Quality-in-Use Model
QM Quality Management
QoS Quality-of-Service
QR-Model Quality Risk Model
QSF Quality Services Factory
QSF readiness check Analysis of an organisation as to whether it is mature for implementing and running a QSF
QSO Quality Service Outcome
QSR Quality Service Request
Quality Gate Checkpoint in a lifecycle to evaluate quality characteristics
ReqQMod Requirements Quality Model
Rel Release
Residual error rate The number of all errors found in validation, verification and production during the first month after go-live divided by the sum of errors found during validation and verification; usually counting will be on blocking and serious errors
RID Report identification number
Risk level Degree of Uncertainty
RiSSQ Right Software and Systems Quality
ROI Return on Investment
RTCA Radio Technical Commission for Aeronautics; a US based organisation

SAGA Standards and Architectures for e-Government Applications
SAP Systemanalyse und Programmentwicklung or Systeme, Anwendungen und Produkte in der Datenverarbeitung; a German based Company
Scrum A framework for effective team collaboration on complex projects
SEI Software Engineering Institute; a US based organisation
SEPA Single Euro Payments Area
Service cluster A number of services with similar properties grouped together
SID Service Identification Number
SIG Special Interest Group
SLA Service Level Agreement
SLA-ID Service Level Agreement Identification Number
SPICE Software Process Improvement and Capability Determination
SQuaRE Systems and software engineering – Systems and software Quality Requirements and Evaluation
SQS Software Quality Systems; a German based company
SQS PractiQ A global corporate standard for all our SQS consultants
SSQ Systems and software quality
ST Systems Test
STD Standard
SUP Supporting Services
Sys System
SysQMod System quality model
System malfunction Not properly working system
T&M Time and Material
TCO Total Cost of Ownership
Temenos Banking software solution; also the Swiss based company developing the software
TestSPICE Software Process Improvement and Capability Determination for Test Processes
TMMI Test Maturity Model Integration
TMap Test Management approach
TOGAF The Open Group Architecture Framework
UAT User Acceptance Test
UML Unified Modelling Language
US United States (of America)
V&V Verification and Validation
V&V order Assignment to the QSF for executing a service based on given assets and values
Value Concrete benefit which can be used and produced by a service
VM-XT V-Modell XT
WD Working days (usually eight hours a day)
WSDL Web Services Description Language
Y2K Year 2000
Zachman framework An enterprise architecture framework which provides a formal and highly structured way of viewing and defining an enterprise

Printing and Binding: Stürtz GmbH, Würzburg